D1297647

# ALL HIS
# FATHER'S SINS

# ALL HIS FATHER'S SINS

## Inside the Gerald Gallego Sex-Slave Murders

Lt. Ray Biondi and Walt Hecox

Bruce B. Henderson, Editor

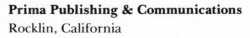
**Prima Publishing & Communications**
Rocklin, California

Typography: Ad Type Graphics
Production: Bookman Productions
Editors: Bruce B. Henderson
Jacket Design: The Dunlavey Studio


Prima Publishing & Communications
Rocklin, CA

**Library of Congress Cataloging-in-Publication Data**

Biondi, Ray.
    All his father's sins: inside the Gerald Gallego sex-slave
murders / Ray Biondi and Walter Hecox.
    p.        cm.
    Revised. Originally published: Monterey, Calif.: Angel
Press, 1986.
    ISBN 0-914629-34-4 : $15.95
    1. Gallego, Gerald.  2. Crime and criminals — United
States — Biography.  3. Murder — United States — Case
studies.  4. Sex crimes — United States — Case studies. I. Hecox, Walter. II. Title.
HV6248.G27B56  1987      *5. Williams, Charlene*
364.1'523'0924 — dc19
[B]  *B10*                                    87-15658
                                               CIP

91 90 89 88    RRD    10 9 8 7 6 5 4 3 2 1

Printed in the United States of America

This book is dedicated to Kippi Vaught, Rhonda Scheffler, Brenda Judd, Sandra Colley, Stacy Redican, Karen Twiggs, Linda Aguilar, Virginia Mochel, Mary Beth Sowers, Craig Miller, and their families.

Special recognition and thanks are offered to District Attorney Richard Wagner and Sheriff Kay McIntosh of Pershing County, Nevada; Investigators John Compston and Tom Moots of the Nevada Bureau of Investigation; and Investigator Frank Dale of the Sacramento County District Attorney's Office.

The hard work and expertise of the other peace officers, criminalists, and technicians who helped solve these crimes and prepare the case for trial can be clearly seen in the following pages.

We are grateful to all.

Behold, all souls are mine; as the soul of the
father, so also the soul of the son is mine:
The soul that sinneth, it shall die.

If he beget a son that is a robber,
a shedder of blood and . . .
Now, lo, if he beget a son that seeth
all his father's sins which he hath done . . .
doth not the son bear the iniquity of the father?

Ezekiel 18: 4, 10, 14 and 19

# The Father

*Two cops and two M.P.'s came up and wanted to know if I was the driver, whereupon I answered them by letting go a couple of fast rights, and two of them went down. I ran several blocks but was soon captured. I was beaten into unconsciousness. I remained in jail for a period of two weeks and then my supervisor came down and got me out. I returned to work, but later my buddy and I quit, and we hauled for Sacramento, California. We arrived there around 7:30 that morning, September 11, 1945. We were hungry so we found a cafeteria and had breakfast. Before being seated, I happened to see two young girls sitting by themselves, so I nudged my buddy, and we took our trays over there and sat down and started talking to them. We learned that they were low on money, so we treated them to breakfast. After the breakfast, we went out of our way trying to help them find jobs, but to no avail. After about three hours of this running around, my buddy suggested we go swimming. We bought the girls bathing suits but never did go swimming, for the girl sitting on my lap, her name was Lorraine, came right out and asked me to marry her. I said I would. We were married a few hours later. To this day, my wife and I are still married but we have been separated for some time now.*

From the death row statement of Gerald Albert Gallego
Mississippi State Prison
Jackson, Mississippi, 1954

A baby boy was born of this union on July 17, 1946. The son was named Gerald Armand Gallego.

# One

The killing started late in the summer of 1978.

Gerald Armand Gallego awoke early on the morning of September 11th. Sacramento was sizzling as it often is at that time of the year. Gallego contemplated the day ahead. There would be girls in the shopping centers and on the streets — tender, barefoot, teen-age girls, tan and lovely in their tank tops and short shorts.

As his desires stirred that morning, Gallego might well have been thinking about Sally Jo, his daughter. His little Sally Jo, who had become his first sex slave long before the gentle fingers of puberty began to mold her breasts and fashion questions in her child's mind.

Even before getting out of bed, he began to think the time had come to turn his latest fantasy into reality. He glanced at the young woman sleeping beside him. She was petite, tiny almost, even childlike. She would help him. She would do anything he told her to do. He was sure of that because she always did. Looking at her, he made his decision.

"This is the day," he announced as he rolled out of bed. "This is the day we make it come true."

Charlene Williams opened her eyes and looked at her lover, whom she thought of as the only man for her. She knew that the first time she saw him sitting at the poker table in a dingy card room, running the game and, no doubt, cheating.

Though it had been almost a year ago to the day, she remembered the night they met as if it were yesterday. The poker club had been strange to her, sleazy, cheap, and frayed at the edges. It was not like any place she'd been before, not at all like the plush gambling casinos in Reno and Lake Tahoe she'd visited with her family. She had ended up in the poker club and with Gerry because of a blind date she had wanted no part of. But she had eventually agreed to the matchmaking because there were times in her life when she wasn't able to say no, not to friends and not to family. So, she had entered the club with her girlfriend. As they walked to a table in the cramped cocktail lounge that adjoined the card room, a combo played western tunes badly enough to torture Charlene's discerning ears.

Just as they sat down, she spotted him. She knew even before her friend pointed him out that the poker dealer was her date. And Charlene, at that instant, decided she liked the idea. There was something about him, something sexual, something wild and powerful, that blinded her immediately.

As soon as Gerry looked at Charlene, the flaws in his rugged features faded. And there *were* flaws. A birthmark on his face marred his well-chiseled, masculine profile. His hair was parted on one side and slicked back on the other in a style popular in the 1920s. And there was a hint of cruelty that lay behind his dark, brooding eyes. But she looked beyond all that. He was a man's man — her kind of macho man. They met, said hello, held hands momentarily, and within two weeks he had worked his way firmly into her life.

Looking up at him now as he stood beside the bed, she realized the cruelty she had initially overlooked was really there. The love pats of their early days had become vicious elbow jabs in the ribs and powerful open-handed slaps which almost knocked her over. In bed, he was an animal, intent only on satisfying himself. He introduced her to lascivious exercises that strained her imagination. And always, there were the fantasies — the filthy images he talked about to increase his excitement.

8

Not quite the five-foot-seven he claimed to be, Gerry carried himself with a strutting arrogance that matched neither his size nor his appearance. At the same time, he could, when he wanted to, drop the bluff and turn on a pleasant and personable manner, winning him friends of both sexes.

Despite Gerry's faults — or maybe because of them — Charlene grew to love him. She planned to be his woman for as long as he wanted her. But lately, since losing his last job and after learning of her pregnancy, he seemed to lose interest in her. These days, he talked more and more about his fantasy, his impossible, lewd fantasy.

Times had changed for Charlene Williams in the last decade. Everybody's good little girl was gone. Actually, she had started disappearing when she was thirteen and attending Rio Americano, the neighborhood high school for the offspring of Sacramento suburbia's upper-middle-class. The leadership role Charlene had assumed in the later grades of elementary school began to slip away during her freshman year in high school. Attracted to a group of campus rebels, she soon became acquainted with marijuana, speed, alcohol, and sex. She was almost kicked out of school, and she would have been had she not been precocious enough to earn sufficient credits for her diploma. Her future was still bright when she married Craig, sweet, innocent, giving Craig. Then came her first divorce and second marriage to Gary. Lazy, parasitical, heroin-shooting Gary should have been at the bottom of her downhill slide. Even then, the good days were still within reach. As always, Daddy was there to give her whatever she wanted, as were Grandma and Mother. After she ended her second marriage, they were there in Carmichael, a Sacramento suburb, waiting for her with open arms.

On September 11, 1978, the good times were further away than ever. Charlene had already taken a dangerously wrong turn when she fell in love with Gerald Gallego. And within hours — by nightfall, to be exact — everything would be gone. Out of reach. Forever. Not even Daddy would be able to save her.

And now this man, this man she knew was the only man for her, said he was ready to fulfill his fantasy. Charlene didn't believe him. How could she believe him? He couldn't be serious. What Gerry wanted was a harem, a cache of slave girls, young and delectable, who would do anything he wanted any time he wanted it.

Charlene had been with Gerry long enough by then to know he wanted a lot. But how in God's name could he bring himself to do it? *Of course* she didn't believe he would do it. After all, fantasies are to be acted out only in the privacy of one's imagination. Certainly they are never meant to become reality.

Gerry made plans as he showered and dressed that morning. He told her what they would do. They would take the van, the big, almost-like-new van. Daddy had never intended it to be used for anything except transportation when he co-signed the loan. But then, Daddy also didn't particularly like the landscape scene painted on the van's sides that Gerry found so attractive: a stark, unearthly mountainous landscape guarded by an evil-looking, hump-backed vulture perched atop a peak and peering down on still more scavengers circling through a blue-gray sky, as if they had scented the odor of death.

They would go to a big shopping center, Gerry explained. There would be young girls, very young girls, the younger the better, strolling through the promenade, dressed for Sacramento's searing September heat — delicious dollies, supple and succulent — hips swaying as they strolled in sandals over hot concrete sidewalks; buttocks peeking beneath the hems of shorts; small, perky breasts hardly covered by scanty halters. Gerry didn't drool when he talked about his would-be slaves, but the effect was the same.

Charlene thought it was all a test, a plan to see if she loved Gerry as much as she claimed, to see if she was up to the standard set by "the girl with heart." Gerry, once admiring another woman from afar, had said, "There's a girl with heart." Charlene had felt a pang of envy, wanting to be that girl. By now, though, Charlene knew "the girl with heart" was not any one woman but another of his fantasies — a female montage pasted together in Gerry's mind, a blending of the best bodies and personalities of the women he had known. There was a rating system for the women in his life, and he kept Charlene informed about her place on the list. Depending on his moods, she ranged from number two to the bottom of the standings. Never was she number one. Never had she yet been equal to "the girl with heart." She wondered if she would ever be worthy of his companionship, his love, of someday even becoming his wife. And she desperately wanted to win the top position. Now, the test was at hand.

They rode in the van to Country Club Plaza in Sacramento. As he drove, Gerry talked more about his plans. Charlene, sitting beside him, kept thinking it wasn't real, that it would stop any time. Any moment now, he would smile and say, "Well, you passed the test. You were willing to go along with it. You're my girl with heart." And it would be over and they would go have lunch.

But Gerry turned into the parking lot and, while looking for a parking place, began giving her instructions. He told her how to pick out the right girls and get them to the van. He stopped at a five-and-dime store to buy tape, two-inch wide adhesive he said would be good for bindings and gags.

Still she didn't believe it was happening, not then, not later, except perhaps in some deep recess of her subconscious where she had made a habit of hiding from reality. It wasn't happening. It simply was not. People didn't do these things. When Gerry told her he would wait in the van while she found the girls, it was just part of the act.

She left the van and wandered alone through the mall, looking at new shoes and dresses in the windows. She loved dresses and always wore them when she could, even though Gerry preferred her to dress in miniskirts and tight pants.

Then she started noticing the young girls.

The morning aged as the blistering Sacramento Valley sun mounted steadily higher in a brassy sky. There were girls, lots of girls, wearing shorts and T-shirts and halters and tank tops,

11

walking on tender and innocent baby legs over sidewalks that were beginning to sizzle. Morning waned and the temperature rose as the afternoon assaulted Country Club Plaza.

Then Gerry was at her side, snarling, growling, a rutting animal scenting sex, telling her she was destroying his plans.

"You're fucking it up," he hissed.

He was outraged and insulted that she was not doing her job, not helping him with his plan, his obscene fantasy, his rapacious obsession. While he talked, he walked by her side through the mall and pointed to a pair of youngsters, children in women's bodies who were standing just outside a fast food restaurant that specialized in hot dogs.

"Get them," he ordered. "They're the two I want. Get them to the van and I'll take over from there."

He melted into the afternoon flow of pedestrian traffic. Charlene walked toward the girls. Incredibly, she convinced them to follow her to the van. Charlene was good at following instructions. She could do anything, remember anything, untangle any puzzle, and more than anything else, she could be led anywhere by any man she accepted as her master. Like the genie in the bottle, she not only obeyed orders, she produced results.

Thinking about how best to complete her task instead of what the result would be, she led the girls to the van. Kippi Vaught and Rhonda Scheffler, one of them sixteen, the other seventeen, were pretty girls with the extra glow that youth always finds in the heat of summer. They were girls who looked a little bit like Charlene, just as she looked a bit like Sally Jo.

As she walked next to the girls, Charlene's camera-like memory photographed them. They both wore tight Levis. One had long brown hair falling over a striped sweater. The other one was more full-bodied, and her hair, long like her companion's, was also brown. They both smiled a lot, and their bodies wiggled in the unaffected way young girls carry themselves. They blended with the late summer scenery, moving parts of a youthful, shifting tableau, noticeable, but not noticed, an attractive frame in a pretty motion picture.

Kippi and Rhonda were close enough to Charlene's age so they would feel a bond with her. At twenty, Charlene was still almost a teen-ager herself. She spoke their language and knew what words to use.

Charlene offered them pot and they went with her. Kippi and Rhonda followed their guide to the van where Charlene opened the rear door and asked them to come in and sit down. As soon as they were settled, the door opened again and they were face to face with Gerald Armand Gallego, who asked them to stay as he engraved his invitation with a nasty little gun he held in his right hand. It was a .25 caliber automatic, small, as handguns go, though its bore must have looked like a cannon to the girls.

None of it was real to Charlene. It was a charade, a dream, a kaleidoscope of horror she watched but could not feel. Gerry issued orders and he went to work. He forced the girls to lie face down on the floor of the van, then bound them, hand and foot, with the tape. He told Charlene to make sure the newly recruited love slaves kept quiet, so she moved to the back of the van and sat on an ice chest.

Gerry started the van and drove out of the parking lot through the side streets to Interstate 80 where he turned east toward the Sierra Nevada.

Charlene sat quietly on the ice chest. She was numb. All of her senses had suddenly hibernated so that she would not remember if the girls cried or screamed or begged. Later, she would prefer to think there were no screams, no sobs, no whimpering. That was her security blanket, her refuge from reality.

There was fear mirrored in the eyes of the teen-agers. Real terror. Charlene could see that when she looked, but still she didn't believe it was happening. Gerry was playing a game. These girls were in on it with him. It had to be that way. Hadn't he pointed them out at the mall? That was because he knew them. He had set the whole show up as part of the test.

This was not a kidnapping. Not a real kidnapping. Charlene would never be involved in anything like that. She would never be a party to such a crime. No one she knew would ever have had anything to do with a kidnapping.

The van rolled on, and the highway began to rise at Penryn, gently at first, then steeply past Newcastle and Auburn and up the heavily muscled slopes of the Sierra Nevada to Baxter. The rounded hills were steeper; the rolling savannah of the foothills was swallowed by steeper slopes. Clumps of live oak rose from a well-browned carpet of wild barley. The dying grass, which withered as the searing sun of early September baked California's Mother Lode country one last time, was replaced by a forest. There, files of tall pine trees marched in helter-skelter columns toward the lofty timber line. Autumn nibbled at the edge of the heat wave. The air cooled as it thinned in the higher altitude.

Baxter is a highway maintenance station for the scores of workers who keep Interstate 80 open through summer's ceaseless stream of traffic and winter's strangling blizzards. It is the snow line, where chains must be used by winter travelers in order to continue their journey through the mountains.

It is the place where an obscene fantasy turned to reality for Gerald Armand Gallego. And the place where Charlene Williams turned down her final chance for redemption.

Gerry turned off the highway at Baxter, shifting gears as he guided the van up a twisting frontage road, across an overpass that traversed the broad highway and on to an area where the pines closed tightly around the two lanes of pavement and a steep, sloping meadow opened beside the road. There he parked the car and turned his attention to the girls. He freed their ankles and ordered them to walk away from the road into the shadows of the pines which bordered the tiny clearing. He told Charlene to wait while he followed them. Gerry carried with him the little gun, a blanket, and a sleeping bag. He was gone a long time.

Charlene waited. Quietly. Patiently. Refusing to believe what her senses were absorbing but her mind would not accept. It wasn't real, she told herself. Pretty soon, Gerry and

14

the girls would show up laughing at the great joke and he would compliment Charlene because she was truly his girl with heart.

Hours passed and the day melted into evening as a chilly wind, born above the timber line on the brow of a distant glacier, tumbled down the slopes and shattered the leading edge of the heat wave. Charlene waited, telling herself more lies, wrestling with reality and rejecting it completely.

Gerald returned alone. He gave her brisk, brief, confident orders. She should take the van back to Sacramento, driving exactly 55 miles an hour so as not to attract the attention of a highway patrolman. Once in Sacramento, though, she was to make sure she was seen with the van by someone, by anyone. Then she was to get her silver-blue Oldsmobile and drive back to the mountains. She would arrive in Baxter at exactly midnight, drive off the ramp as Gerry had and pick him and the girls up in the forest. A signal was arranged with horn and headlights so Gerry would know she was there.

"It will take you exactly an hour to drive down and an hour back," Gerry told her. "Don't go any faster or any slower. Take your time while you are there. Be seen. And be back here at midnight."

He was concerned, wondering if she could handle the van by herself. But she knew she could. She learned quickly and was good with cars, good at almost anything she put her mind to.

Charlene drove back down the mountain, out of autumn and back into summer where heat haze shimmered and shook over the valley. She drove almost all the way back to the Country Club Plaza where it had all started. She visited a friend for a few minutes and was seen driving the van. Then she changed cars, taking the Olds back into the mountains where Gerry waited in a night which was becoming frigid.

Charlene did not even think of calling the police. She drove on, blindly following orders, right or wrong, as she had all her life. She drove back to the mountains but arrived too soon. Afraid to be early, she parked at the turnoff, anxious not to displease her man.

Fate or luck or whatever whimsical spirit was riding with Charlene that night offered her a final chance for redemption. A black and white police car arrived in Baxter and prowled to and fro curiously. Charlene watched it with trepidation. She could not tell whether the car was driven by a highway patrolman, a sheriff's deputy, or some local constable, and she did not care to find out. She did not flag down the police car and report what was happening to the girls. She did not attempt to save their lives. Instead, she started the car's engine and drove up the frontage road, crossing the highway as Gerry had, and followed the route he had taken to the tiny clearing. There, she parked and signaled him.

Gerry appeared in a few seconds and brushed off her apology for being early.

"It's okay, I was freezing my ass off," he replied. He got into the car and told her to drive into the woods, then he got out and came back with the girls. He put them in the back seat at gun point. Kippi and Rhonda showed signs of their ordeal. Their clothes were stained and dirty. Their faces were pale and drawn. Once carefully groomed long hair was matted with bark and pine needles. They sat in the back seat and Gerry climbed in next to them, patting their legs and assuring them everything would be all right.

"We're just going to take you out in the country," he said casually. "Some place where you can't get to the police too fast."

The conversation was perfectly pleasant, Charlene noticed, except the girls' voices were strained, on the edge of hysteria.

Charlene drove, at Gerry's instructions, down the mountain again, 55 miles an hour and no faster. As they approached Sacramento, he ordered her to drive through to the south until she finally reached the Old Jackson Road, not far from Sloughhouse on the other side of town.

Gerry was jovial on the return drive, talking, laughing, joking, having a party which only he was enjoying. Through the numb confusion which had gripped and held her all day,

Charlene realized he was trying to make the girls feel at ease. He explained to them, more than once, that nothing bad would happen to them. They were just taking them to a place which would make it hard for them to get back to civilization and a telephone.

Of course, something dreadfully bad had already happened to the girls. They had been ravished, violated, forced to submit to all the facets of his twisted lust. But now, he looked into their blank stares and assured them they would not be harmed.

Charlene listened. He must mean it. He wouldn't kill them. She could not picture what he might have done to them in the wilderness.

She drove on. Following Gerry's instructions, she stopped carefully at intersections, even though not a human being, not a light in the darkness of the wee hours, was visible anywhere.

"Don't take any chances," he warned her.

He talked nicely to the girls but sternly to Charlene. One minute she was going too fast. Then, when she used the brake to keep the car at a crawl, he found fault again.

"Don't ride the brakes!"

Then, "Slow down!"

He ordered her to turn left and kill the headlights, warning her to watch for ditches at the roadside as she drove along. Eventually, they crossed the steel rails of a cattle guard.

"Pull over here," he commanded.

Music was playing on the car radio. The strains recorded themselves dimly on Charlene's mind.

Gerry and the well-built girl got out of the car. She was nice-looking, Charlene thought in a detached way, but not really Gerry's type. Then they were gone, off into the dark field. Charlene was chatting, telling the slender girl in the back that everything would be fine. Gerry wouldn't hurt her. And then Gerry was back, alone.

"Turn the music up all the way," he snapped.

Charlene obeyed, and pulsating music shattered the silent night.

"Don't turn around," he warned. "Don't look." Gerry took the second girl with him and Charlene sat in the car, frozen in place. She heard popping noises and saw flashes nearby. All of it happened in a few seconds, then Gerry was back at the car, standing at the driver's window, breathing heavily and telling her to move over.

She scooted across the seat and he sat beside her, looking straight ahead, his expression cold and immobile. His voice was calm and deliberate.

"One of them is still wiggling," he said.

Charlene held her breath momentarily.

He got out of the car and there were more popping noises. When the girl who had been wiggling stopped, he returned to the car.

Gerry drove then, winding the Olds over the country road back to Sacramento and their apartment. They rode in silence and entered the apartment without speaking. Gerry sat down on the couch. He motioned to her to sit beside him, then urged her to sit even closer. When she did, he put his arm around her waist, encircling her slender body and then rubbing the back of her hand with his. He touched her gently and started to say something, but she interrupted him.

"I'm glad you did it," Charlene said. "I was afraid I was going to have to."

\*       \*       \*

Two days later the September heat wave ended, as it often does in Sacramento, with the first soothing rains of autumn. The trailing edge of a tropical storm had drifted north from the Baja coast, bringing with it scudding clouds which mottled the evening sky and now and then splattered the thirsty dust with a warm drizzle.

Alfredo Oregal and his friend, Samuel Ochoa, walked through the damp evening along the lane which branches off Meiss Road to the Silva farm near Sloughhouse. The sun had set and twilight was dimming under the cloud cover as night hurried in from the east.

18

Death was no stranger to the two Mexican nationals employed as hired hands on the Silva farm. Alfredo was startled but not frightened when he saw the still figure lying in the meadow just off the farm road. He walked over the damp, dead grass to within a few feet of the body and stood there for a moment, absorbing his discovery.

The dead person was a young woman with pretty features and long hair that fanned out over the wild barley. She was lying on her back and the dark stains under her head looked like blood. All of the color had drained from her face. The features were rigid and motionless, an unfinished wax doll staring back at him with fixed pupils through the dimming light.

Alfredo returned to Samuel and told him the woman was dead. They hurried back to the farm and told Enrique Oregal, the only member of the farm crew who spoke English. Enrique listened to Alfredo's account of what he had seen in the clearing, and they all went to the barn where they knew Olaf Anderson, the farm mechanic, was still working.

Olaf joined the group, which crowded into Enrique's car. He drove back along the farm road, through the gathering darkness to the place where Alfredo said he'd seen the body.

When the car stopped, they all got out and followed Alfredo, who was carrying a flashlight. They walked forward until the beam of light picked out a form lying on the grass. Then they paused, at the same time curious and respectful of the dead.

They all stood there for a short time longer, within inches of the murdered girl, staring. She was so young, so pretty, so utterly lifeless lying there on the seared grass that carpeted the surface of the meadow.

Suddenly, Alfredo cried out, "This isn't the body I found!"

# TWO

*Lt. Ray Biondi — Homicide*

I'm not going to tell you a tale of heroism. No one man or woman was responsible for solving the shocking crimes depicted in this account. Instead, I'm going to share with you the challenges inherent in any unsolved murder case. But more important, you'll learn of the difficulties experienced by the authorities in three states in their efforts to end the brutal spree of kidnappings, rapes, and murders committed by Charlene and Gerald Gallego.

When the call came in to the homicide unit of the Sacramento County Sheriff's Department, we had already been investigating the case of the two missing young women. Seldom is a missing persons case referred to homicide so soon, but the first tidbits of information about the disappearances of Kippi Vaught and Rhonda Scheffler were so disturbing that we were notified within hours of Leonard Scheffler's report.

It would turn out that some of the information we developed — not only early in the investigation but also much later — was wrong, completely and terribly wrong. Nevertheless, we were led to one correct assumption. From the facts we had available in those first few days, we believed there was a better than even chance the two missing girls were dead.

When the two bodies were found in a meadow near Sloughhouse, I had been in charge of the homicide detail for

21

two years. This has often surprised me, since unlike many of my police colleagues, I never deliberately directed my life toward a career in law enforcement.

I grew up in a remote California town located in one of the high desert valleys in the Sierra Nevada. As a young man, I had no intention of leaving what I considered God's country. I married the girl next door, Carol, and together we survived some rough winters when the seasonal jobs in the woods ended. Beautiful country or not, I needed steady work. I went to Sacramento and took so many civil service exams that I lost count. When several job offers came in, I selected the sheriff's office because it sounded like the most challenging. Little did I realize then how this decision would alter my life forever.

The farm mechanic's call reached the sheriff's department at about 8:30 p.m. on September 13th. I was at home eating a late dinner when the watch commander called me. Only moments before, I had walked in the door after a long day working on the disappearances of Kippi and Rhonda.

I got up from the table and said my goodbyes to Carol and our five sons. I knew I would not be home again for days.

Homicide investigations should not move slowly. Witnesses, clues, and even physical evidence are all often mobile, elusive, and forgetful. Blood cells are breaking down each moment they wait for laboratory analysis. Fingerprints are smudged, footprints are lost, and memories fade. My habit is to assign every man available in the opening stages of an investigation so that as little as possible is lost during the crucial early hours. On a fresh homicide, it's not uncommon for us to work two or three days and nights straight, fortified by black coffee and occasional catnaps at our desks.

En route to the crime scene, I radioed the department dispatcher and asked that my detectives be contacted at home. I had specific assignments for some, and others I wished to have join me at the scene. Because we had been investigating the missing persons report and interviewing witnesses, we were all familiar with the details of the case. In my mind, I went over what we had already done and thought about Leonard Scheffler, Rhonda's nineteen-year-old husband, whom I had interviewed the previous day.

Leonard told me that at 4:10 p.m. on the afternoon of the 11th he'd arrived home puzzled because his wife had failed to pick him up from work. He had called Kippi Vaught's mother, and she also became worried. Leonard and Mrs. Vaught waited, at first impatiently, then anxiously. Eventually, they went to the Country Club Plaza because Leonard knew that's where Rhonda was planning to shop. He and Mrs. Vaught fanned out. Leonard found Rhonda's Subaru parked in the north section of the plaza. He turned the key in the ignition and the car started up with no trouble. In the trunk, he found packages from various stores in the mall. The concerned husband and mother questioned employees in the stores nearby. Before long, they picked up the trail. The clerks at a couple of stores remembered the pretty young girls who had made purchases. At a shoe store, Leonard learned that Rhonda had returned a pair of shoes about three o'clock that afternoon. Leonard had returned home and the hours passed. Eight o'clock. Nine o'clock. Still no Rhonda or any word from her. It just wasn't like her. At 10:10 p.m., Leonard had called the sheriff's department and the two girls became missing persons.

The next day, Kippi Vaught's mother admitted to detectives that her daughter had been a runaway in the past but claimed she had been doing well lately. No personal items or clothing belonging to Kippi were missing from the house, as they had been when she had run away previously.

The case of the two missing young women was made public after Leonard visited a local television station on September 12th and enlisted their help in the search. At that point, we began getting the inevitable calls reporting possible sightings.

Through the 12th and 13th, we occupied ourselves with the tedious details involved in any investigation. We separated, as best we could, the wheat from the chaff in the telephone tips, traced the girls' movements step by step through the 11th, and talked to almost every employee in the Country Club Plaza. We talked to all the members of the Vaught and Scheffler families who lived in the Sacramento area. We heard about the missing girls' good habits and their bad ones.

A remark about Rhonda's life insurance was called to our attention. But we were told repeatedly by friends and relatives that the Schefflers had a good marriage, despite their youth. Her friends said Rhonda would never walk away from her marriage but would face any problems, if there were any, in an open and forthright manner. Apparently, they quarreled, like most married couples, but never seriously. Both girls attended Vista Nueva High School, and we learned they were average students with no discipline problems. Both of them had attended all of their classes on the 11th.

We heard about every strange-acting and suspicious-looking character who had been anywhere near the Country Club Plaza that day. A clerk in a drugstore told us she had seen the two young women with a Latin-type man at four o'clock. Other people swore they had seen the teen-agers hitchhiking fifty miles away in Placer County. Someone else said they were seen riding in a car in El Dorado County near Lake Tahoe. Of course, Kippi and Rhonda were not in any of those places.

Driving down the farm lane in the dark, I saw a beehive of cars and lights ahead and knew I was there. I did a quick mental re-check. Did I make all the necessary assignments? Does my pocket recorder have fresh batteries?

A modern-day homicide investigator's critical piece of equipment, I'm convinced, is not his gun but his tape recorder. Details must be recorded at the scene. Interviews with witnesses must be dictated. Each step of the investigation needs to be documented. Reminders of things to do should be dictated immediately before they are forgotten. We spend more time talking to that little machine than we do with our partners.

Other police paraphernalia — guns, handcuffs, spare bullets, and so forth — are things which tend to pull at your waistband and stick in your side while bending over a body or digging in the dirt for an empty shell casing, so I generally don't even bother carrying a gun. Some of my fellow officers have commented about this habit of mine, and a few of them don't approve. I have learned, though, that the least intimidating approach is usually the most effective way to get information from witnesses and suspects.

I looked for a place to park on the narrow road now crowded with a dozen cars, some belonging to cops and some to reporters. There were the inevitable television equipment trucks with antennae pointed downtown so that a live report could make the eleven o'clock news.

There is a lot of activity at the scene when a murder victim is found. Barricades are put up, photographs taken, evidence collected, and witnesses interviewed. In spite of all the activity, the early stages of a homicide investigation are, for me, mostly mental.

I always find it necessary to remind myself not to react to the obvious, to remain objective. Nothing is taken for granted except that the victim is dead. In most cases, the actual cause of death and sequence of how things happened are rarely ever close to the first theories offered. Such theories often make killers seem smarter and more sophisticated than they really are.

I took a flashlight and walked down to where the bodies had been found. They had been photographed but, so far, not disturbed. I compared physical descriptions as well as the clothes the girls were wearing when they disappeared, and I was soon convinced of their identity.

I returned to my car. Ignoring the shouted questions from the media, I picked up my radio mike and put out a call for my detectives to "make contact." I was determined that the two girls' parents and Rhonda's husband not hear about the grisly discovery from the news media, so I had stationed detectives to stand by in the neighborhoods of the relatives. Now, after receiving my message, my men would be knocking on doors with the tragic news. The relatives would be told that, pending X-rays and dental chart analyses, we were 99 percent sure that their loved ones had been found dead.

I hate this part of my job.

# Three

Charlene sat beside Gerry in the apartment. She looked up at him demurely, like a college girl on a date with a big man on campus, and asked him how he had ended the lives of Rhonda Scheffler and Kippi Vaught.

He told her it was all right. He'd knocked them unconscious with a tire iron before he shot them. "Believe me," he said, "they never knew what happened."

Later, they searched through the girls' purses. There was a roach clip in one, an apparatus used to hold a stick of marijuana. Gerry examined it for a moment, then tossed it back into the purse.

"Drugs will get you in trouble," he said with a pious air that suggested what happened to the girls was their own fault.

They slept a little. When they rose in the morning, they agreed it was important to dispose of the clothes Gerry had been wearing the night before. Charlene remembered that the blue and white shirt with western-style cuffs and corduroy trousers was the same outfit he'd been wearing the night they met.

They drove to a dumpster behind a nearby discount department store and left the clothes in a pile of debris. From there, they went to Gerry's aunt's house. Knowing she would be at work, he went directly into a shed at the rear of the house. There, he produced the little .25 caliber revolver which he'd used to kill Rhonda and Kippi. Using a small anvil that was part of a vise attached to the work bench, Gerry pounded flat the nose of the little gun.

He then drove along the banks of the Sacramento River not far from the airport and stopped the car where the river flows around a sweeping bend. Getting out of the car and standing by a steep bank, he dropped the deadly little gun into one of the purses and threw it into the river.

"The gun will weigh down the purse so no one will find it," Gerry explained, sounding smug and tutorial. He then put dirt and rocks in the second purse and threw it into the river.

Gerry opened the trunk of the Oldsmobile and Charlene saw the tire iron for the first time, lying on a rag. Most of one end was stained by a liquid that had dried to a rusty, orange color. Charlene thought it was orange paint.

"That's blood," Gerry explained. "That's what it looks like dried."

He threw anything that might connect them with the murders into the river. Then they returned to the apartment. Gerry began to make preparations for a trip to Oregon, and Charlene, two months pregnant, prepared herself for a grim interlude at an abortion clinic before they left.

A casual atmosphere dominated the waiting room in the abortion clinic. Women and girls, most of them about Charlene's age, were sitting around with cups in their hands, chatting as if they were at a coffee klatch. Charlene, tight-lipped, watched them until her name was called.

When the procedure was over, Charlene started cramping badly. She was instructed to lie still on the table. She had rested there only a short time when Gerry came into the room. "What's holding you up?" he inquired. "We've got to get going."

Charlene stood up obediently and walked on unsteady legs to the van. Gerry helped her, warning her as she went: "You can't act sick like this when we get to Chico," he said. "Remember, we're going to stop there on the way back and see my family."

Driving north to Oregon, they followed the coast to Gold Beach and Wedderburn at the mouth of the Rogue River, where they stayed with friends and were going to get married. But when Gerry discovered they would have to wait several days in Oregon for a license, he changed his mind about the wedding.

Charlene took the change in plans bitterly but without comment. She had long since discovered the best way to be hit by an elbow in the ribs was to argue with Gerry. They drove back to California almost immediately, stopping at the Chico ranch house of Gallego's mother, Lorraine, which she shared with Gerry's stepfather and grandmother.

Actually, the "ranch house" had once been a barn, constructed to store hay, chicken feed, and livestock. A big relic of a building, it had been converted half-heartedly into a residence. Lorraine dominated the household. She was a strong-willed woman who expected others to cater to her and handle trivial chores like housework. Contesting her supremacy was Gerald's grandmother, who trusted few people but had seemed to like Charlene during earlier visits.

There was also Sally Jo.

At fourteen, Sally Jo was emerging from childhood, although Charlene was not sure childhood was the right word. She wondered if Sally Jo had ever been a child. Even though Gerald's mother and grandmother had tentatively approved of her son's latest woman, it was obvious Sally Jo did not share their opinion. Earlier, the girl had lived with Gerry and Charlene for a short time. Sally Jo had made obvious her dislike for the slender, blonde newcomer whom she considered a rival. Eventually, Charlene had told Gerry that Sally Jo's attitude was intolerable and that either his daughter or she would have to go. Charlene won that round. Until that afternoon in late September, 1978, Charlene had not even tried to analyze the youngster's apparent hatred of her.

Gerry, spotting his stepfather working in the back, headed in that direction. The scene when Charlene entered the house was right out of Dogpatch. As soon as she set foot into the living room, she caught the hostile expression of Gerry's grandmother. Lorraine was kneeling on the floor in the next room, visible through the half-open door, talking agitatedly into the telephone.

"Did you get married?" the grandmother demanded. "Did you? Did you?"

Charlene said she and Gerry had not married.

"Well, it's a good thing," the grandmother said. "There's another woman."

The elderly woman's voice was shrill and her eyes were full of anger. Charlene couldn't understand the change in her attitude since their last visit.

"What are you talking about?" Charlene asked.

The grandmother didn't answer her directly but kept repeating that there was another woman in Gerry's life. When Lorraine hung up the phone, she came into the room and explained they had just learned that Gerry had been having sexual intercourse with Sally Jo for years.

"He needs help," Lorraine said. "He might kill someone if he doesn't get help."

Charlene should have been outraged, angered, repulsed, disgusted with the news. Instead, she stood silently, thinking, *Well, he's already killed.* Then she thought about Sally Jo's attitude toward her, and it all began to make sense.

Why Sally Jo had chosen this time to report her father can only be speculated. But report him she did. She told an investigating officer from the Butte County Sheriff's Department every sordid detail of her father's obscene use of her. One long afternoon in Charlene's car, he'd abused Sally Jo and a teenage girlfriend of hers in every lewd way imaginable. In the cold, impersonal prose of policemen describing a crime, the Butte County Sheriff's report dated September 25, 1978, tells how Sally Jo's father had forced her to have intercourse with him once or twice a week for the past six years. She described their sessions in various locales — at home, in the back of the van, and in the Olds.

Without saying anything, Charlene went back out the front door. She found Gerry in a tool shed in the back, talking with his stepfather. Gerry's stepfather was saying that Lorraine had called the police when she saw them pull up and that they should get going because the cops had a warrant for his arrest for child molestation.

A hectic scene followed. Suddenly, Gerry became terrified. He told Charlene to get into the van. He climbed behind the steering wheel and threw the van into reverse.

There was a rifle and a .38 caliber revolver in the van and, upon his orders, Charlene threw them both into the bushes beside the driveway as the van exploded onto the gravel road in front of the house and sped away.

Gerry didn't drive fast for long. He dropped the speed to well within the limit, and a short time later they passed a policeman in a black and white patrol car parked beside the road. Gerry told Charlene to get into the rear of the van and watch to see if the policeman followed. She sat on the ice chest that had been her seat when they had driven Kippi Vaught and Rhonda Scheffler into the mountains. The police car did not follow them. When they crossed the county line, they checked into a motel.

Gerry was in a mood Charlene had never seen before. He was crying, but there were no tears. Dazed and depressed, he stared almost sightlessly around the motel room. His mood frightened her. For a while, she thought he might kill himself.

Charlene still felt bound to this man, in spite of what she'd just heard from his mother. Anyway, she wasn't sure she had a choice. Charlene was convinced that Gerry would not let her leave him and live. She knew too much. She also knew that she was hopelessly and irrevocably tied to the Vaught-Scheffler murders. If she went to the police and told them what she knew, she, too, would be charged with crimes. Certainly not murder, though. Charlene did not think of herself guilty of murder. Still, it would be unpleasant. There was nothing else to do but stick with Gerry and help him. He was her man, for better or worse.

The atmosphere in the motel room grew grotesque. During the first few hours, Gerry made it clear with every action, every word, that Sally Jo was the woman he loved. His confused

31

and obscene emotions were tied in an incoherent knot around the little girl.

There was no remorse on his part for anything he'd done. Rather, he believed he had been wronged by the woman-child he loved. Sally Jo had betrayed him by turning him in to the police. She ratted on him. That kind of behavior was beyond his comprehension. He talked for a while, then sat and stared into space. Finally, he suggested they go to a nearby bar to get a drink.

The drinks didn't help Gerry's mood. He was nervous and frightened when they returned to the motel room. He looked out the window, his gaze resting on the van, and said, "We can't go anywhere in that." He said they had to get another car. While he stayed behind in the room to write a letter to Sally Jo, Charlene drove the van to Sacramento and picked up the Olds. By the time she returned from the eighty-mile return trip, he had finished the letter.

Gerry wanted to meet with his mother so she could give back to him the $700 he had sent home for Sally Jo. Charlene kept her emotions in check when he talked about the money, but it wasn't easy. Seven hundred dollars! They had been living on the money she earned as a meat cutter. Gerry had always insisted she turn every paycheck over to him. Somehow, he had saved $700 and sent it to Sally Jo. Charlene was appalled.

Gerry did call his mother, and later, they met her at a tavern in Chico. She brought him the money. As they parted, Gerry's mother gripped Charlene's arm and said, "Take care of my boy."

*What a switch!* thought Charlene, remembering that it was his mother who called the sheriff in the first place.

Her family was so different — they were normal, loving people. Long ago, when Charlene was a little girl, they had lived in a modest home in a middle-class residential area of Stockton, California. Charlene's father was a butcher then, employed by a local supermarket, an extraordinary man in an ordinary job. But life had been good; they often entertained guests in their neat, carefully groomed bungalow. One of Charlene's fondest memories of her childhood was overnight stays at her maternal grandparents who lived nearby. Her grandmother was doting the way grandmothers are supposed to be, and Charlene loved her a lot. Everything was in place at her grandmother's — the priceless china in the crystal cabinet, every high-backed chair, each rug and handmade quilt, every side table. Charlene liked dressing up in filmy white dresses with pink satin sashes and dancing while her grandfather played the fiddle. The *Tennessee Waltz* was Charlene's favorite, and she whirled to its strains until the old man tired and put down his instrument. She was a little lady then, everyone's little lady, Daddy's and Grandmother's more than anyone else's, but everyone loved her. She missed them more and more these days.

The next morning, she and Gerald were back in Sacramento exchanging the car for the van because Gerry had changed his mind again. They visited Charlene's parents, who had moved to Carmichael several years earlier. Only her mother was home. As they were watching television with her, the news came on. It was then they learned that two black men were the prime suspects in the investigation of the murders of Rhonda Scheffler and Kippi Vaught.

"They can't do anything now," Gerry jubilantly told Charlene as they drove home. "They've got a pair of black suspects and they're stuck with them."

# Four

*Lt. Biondi — Homicide*

For the moment, Gerald Gallego was right. Our investigation of the murders of Rhonda Scheffler and Kippi Vaught had led us steadily in the wrong direction.

When the coroner examined the two girls, he found a wound behind one corpse's left ear that had been made by a bullet grazing her skull. A second bullet had been fired directly into the back of her head. It was possible, the coroner told me, that the first shot had grazed the girl but had not killed her. None of the blows from a blunt instrument was severe enough to have caused death.

Had the wounded teen-ager not wiggled and caught Gallego's attention, there's a chance she might have lived. She would have been able to tell us about her stocky, arrogant attacker named Gerry and the blonde named Charlene, about the Olds and the van. Had we been able to talk with her, other lives might have been saved. But she *did* move, and Gallego, as cold-blooded as any killer I had ever tried to track down, left the car and stood over her to fire the coup de grace shot into her brain.

Every available facility of the sheriff's department worked on the mystery. Technicians, criminalists, detectives, and beat patrol officers all contributed hundreds of man-hours to the investigation. In examining the habits and routines of the victims, we found two normal, middle-class American girls leading normal lives. We followed one lead after another, looking for the clue that would begin to get us closer to their killer or killers.

On September 14th, Detective Stan Reed, a soft-spoken but tough veteran investigator, took a call that looked, in the beginning, as though it would crack the case wide open. A young woman who would not give her name was on the line.

"I want to make one thing clear," she said. "I don't want this call traced. If it is, I'll never help out again."

"Don't worry, there's no tracing equipment," Reed told her. "It's not that easy. That's TV stuff anyway."

"All right," the young woman said. "The two girls on the news tonight . . . are they still missing?"

"Yes. Why do you ask?"

The young woman went on to say she had been riding with three friends in a pickup truck at the intersection where Country Club Plaza and Country Club Center meet. There, she said, she saw Rhonda and Kippi get into a new maroon Pontiac Firebird or Chevrolet Camaro.

She was positive it was them because she had gone to high school with Kippi and knew her well, she told the detective. She described the driver — a black man with a thick scar on his face, near the nose. He had a black male companion. Both of them had Afro haircuts, one modified more than the other.

Before the conversation ended, Reed was able to convince the girl on the phone to let him speak to her mother. Eventually, an arrangement was made for both of them to be questioned. When they met, the girl told Reed that the pickup had stopped at an intersection near the shopping center, and all four witnesses remembered seeing Rhonda and Kippi getting into the maroon car, and with good reason. One of the girls riding in the back of the pickup had shouted, "Nigger lovers!" when she saw Rhonda and Kippi climbing into the car.

"The tall, slim one with the straighter hair looked at us when she heard that," the driver of the pickup told us. "She didn't say anything back, just looked at us. So I got a real good look at her."

All four witnesses from the pickup identified photographs of the two murdered girls.

We questioned relatives and friends of Kippi's and Rhonda's and asked if either had any black male friends. Kippi, we learned, had become friendly with a young black employee of the Good Samaritan Home for Boys. She had met him when she visited the home with her father who was doing some construction work there.

Kippi's mother said her daughter had developed an interest in social work during the same period and that she had become friendly with the young black man who worked as a counselor at the home. Her mother went on to say that Kippi had then changed her mind and told her that she was no longer interested in that line of work. The young black counselor, meanwhile, was dismissed from his job at the home.

Through the days that followed, we developed evidence which strongly indicated this same young black man was the driver of the maroon car. We learned that he was the owner of a maroon Firebird, which he kept in mint condition. And yet, the car had a scratch on a rear fender at about the height of a cattle guard rail near the field where the bodies were found. Examining the crime scene and the area around it, we discovered what appeared to be some reddish paint on the cattle guard. However, when analyzed, this smear proved to be rust.

From the records at the home where the young man had worked, we discovered he had been fired. He was accused of drinking on the job and of taking the young men under his supervision to his favorite hangouts. They were not the type of establishments the home's management believed would help enhance their program.

We thoroughly investigated the young man and all his associates. Statements were taken from his wife, from whom he was separated, and two girlfriends. He took a polygraph test, which was, as are almost all such tests, "inconclusive." With his consent, his car was searched. Fingerprints found in the car were compared with those taken from the hands of the two murdered girls, but there was no match.

Some of the suspect's friends were positive that he could not have committed murder, pointing out that their friend had never owned a gun and had never been prone to violence. Others disagreed, and at least one of his acquaintances was certain that the former counselor had murdered the girls, but he offered no solid evidence. Many of his friends claimed that the young man confined his dating to white women much younger than he.

The young man did harm to his own cause. The first time we questioned him, he changed his account of his activities on the day in question three times. He also sent one of his girl-friends a note, a parting message which was harshly critical of her for not providing him with an alibi.

Everyone who knew the young man agreed he had only one black friend. We found his friend and learned that he strongly resembled the second man seen in the maroon car.

A few of the people who claimed to have seen the two girls getting into the maroon car selected the former counselor's photograph as that of the driver. Others identified completely different individuals — faces of people included in a photographic lineup who had been securely locked in jail on the day Kippi and Rhonda were kidnapped and murdered.

We answered hundreds of telephone calls and followed scores of clues. By the time Gerald Gallego and Charlene Williams had returned to Sacramento after their trip to Oregon, the former counselor and his friend were our primary suspects.

\*     \*     \*

Even though I live daily with murder, each new case adds an edge of sadness to my life. It's even worse when this sadness is coupled with frustration. My job was to tell the families exactly what had happened to their children. In this case, I would not be able to do that for a long time. The coincidence that linked our black suspects to the murdered girls made the experience doubly frustrating. To this day, every clue available indicates the two young women did indeed ride a short distance in the counselor's maroon Firebird.

If any man is capable of living happily with the murders of two teen-age girls on his conscience, Gallego had every reason to be content at that moment.

# Five

When Gerry learned that Charlene's father had connections in Houston, he insisted they go there until the heat let up. Ironically, it was the sexual abuse warrant that worried him more than the murders in Sacramento. "We'll get married in Reno," he said, contemplating a stopover on their way to Texas.

Charlene was tired of the line. It was the fifth or sixth time since they had been living together that he had promised marriage.

"It will be the last legal thing you ever do," he said, smiling. "I'm going to make a legitimate woman out of you." Of course, marriage was not new to either Charlene or Gerry. He was her third husband and she was his fifth wife.

Gerry and Charlene were married in Reno on September 30, 1978. The day of the wedding was a fiasco. Her parents had been vacationing in Reno, and Charlene, thinking they might still be in town, had called every major hotel and motel in the area. But they were nowhere to be found. Finally, she called her grandmother. An hour later, Mr. and Mrs. Williams returned home to California and were told about Charlene's wedding plans. They turned around and went right back to Reno. Exhausted when they arrived, they had trouble finding the courthouse, but smiling bystanders were more than willing to give them directions. "They thought *we* were getting married," her mother told Charlene.

It was the only time that evening anyone laughed. For Charlene's parents, the impending separation from their only child was traumatic. The goodbyes were tearful. When they reached Houston, Gerry had a job waiting for him, compliments of Charlene's father. But, as usual, Gerry found a supervisor he didn't like, so he quit. He then started bartending in a Houston nightclub.

Gerry decided he needed a new identity because of the California arrest warrant. Skilled in the ways of the underworld, he knew exactly what he had to do to get a new birth certificate. He reached into Charlene's family tree and selected the name of a distant relative whom they knew had been born in Sacramento County. Having convinced Charlene's family that he had been wrongly accused in Chico, Gallego prevailed on her mother to go to the courthouse and get him a copy of the man's birth certificate. Not trusting the document to the mails, she drove to Houston with a friend and hand delivered Gerry's new identity. Ironically, the stolen name belonged to a California State police officer.

Gerry began leading a double life. On the job, he was Stephen Feil, with valid ID to prove it. Among the circle of friends they developed, Gerry and Charlene were the Gallegos.

Charlene, alone in a Houston apartment most of the time, was lonely but relatively content. Life with Gerry was going as smoothly as she could expect. She wanted to get a job and he finally let her. She applied to a bank near their home and was hired immediately. Though Gerry liked the money she brought home, he resented her Midas touch in the business world.

Charlene inherited her talent for business success from her father. About the time she was entering grade school, her father's hard work and social acumen began to pay off. A large Sacramento-based supermarket chain had little trouble convincing the Stockton supermarket butcher to take a job as manager of one of their stores. From there, Chuck Williams' success was phenomenal. A workaholic who was blessed with a personality that charmed men and women alike, Williams rose to the top rapidly. Before many years passed, he was vice president in charge of operations for another supermarket chain whose outlets spanned half the continent.

His daughter walked almost every step up the ladder with him. From the beginning, their relationship was close. He always made time for her and indulged her every whim. He would buy her anything she wanted. They shopped together, ate together, flew in his friend's pleasure aircraft together, and sailed together. She even assumed the duties of acting as her father's hostess, often meeting his business associates in social settings. This role was expanded further when Charlene's mother had an auto accident that left her with an injured back and a limited desire to travel.

Having grown up surrounded by the male culture of her father's business world, Charlene expected and wanted men to dominate. So when Gerry's short-lived role of the gracious, gentlemanly suitor changed to that of a bullying bed partner, she accepted the change as part of the price of being the woman of a man's man.

Charlene never understood what happened next in Houston. Gerry had told her on several occasions that he wanted her to practice to see how fast she could "break the house down and be ready to travel." All the while, he fought with a fellow bartender and was on the verge of losing his job. One day, the inevitable happened. He came home and told her to "break the house down" immediately because they were moving. Charlene never knew why they left so fast.

They ended up back in Reno, and throughout the spring of 1979, Gerry and Charlene took trips across the broad area of the rolling high desert east of the gambling capital. They explored the open range and its cover of sagebrush and stunted juniper, Pyramid Lake, and the Humboldt Sink. Sometimes they teamed up with other couples they'd met and camped beside Lake Lahontan, near Fallon, where they could water ski. Other times they visited long, deserted mine shafts outside of Lovelock, where the Humboldt Sink begins to be a lake and drowns the lowlands beside the tiny city.

Again, Gerry found employment with the help of Chuck Williams and went to work as a driver for a Sparks meat distributor. But soon he quit, or so he told Charlene. She never could be sure of the truth. But she did know one thing. He again became impotent, just as he had in Sacramento when he lost his job.

If life was not easy when Gerry was performing normally, it was nearly impossible when he could not. He demanded that she arouse him and suggested one sexual remedy after another. When nothing worked, he blamed her. And yet, he would force her to try again and again.

Meanwhile, Charlene had walked into another meat company and found work without any assistance from her father. She could do that. Unlike her husband, she had a knack for getting jobs and keeping them.

She also had the ability to make friends with men and enemies of women. Charlene could not understand why the female employees at her new firm seemed to resent her, although she didn't let it worry her much. Frankly, she preferred the company of men, while she felt competitive with women. She made a point of wearing dresses from the extensive and expensive wardrobe she had accumulated over the years, most of which her father had purchased for her. She enjoyed and even encouraged the company of the male employees at work and began disappearing for two-hour lunches with the sales manager. Her relationship with him became one of mental intimacy. For the first time since meeting Gerry, she found another man she enjoyed being with. But Charlene wasn't about to be unfaithful to a man she knew was a killer.

Her attraction to Gerry, which seemed almost hypnotic when they first met, was weakening. Her feelings of fear over what they'd done, however, immobilized her and kept her from leaving. But it went beyond that — Gerry was her man and he always would be. Her feelings for him were primal. She could not imagine life without Gerry, any more than she could imagine life without her father.

Charlene did not believe in the total sanctity of marriage where sex was concerned. She believed that men, all men, were cheaters, and their infidelity was the cross all married women must bear. And she found nothing wrong with taking advantage of the tendency of husbands to stray and play. Before Gerry, she'd enjoyed many sessions of bedroom badminton with a married man. But since taking up with Gerry, she had been faithful to him. His demands on her time and his overpowering sexual obsession didn't leave room for anyone else.

Some of Gerry and Charlene's camping trips into the chaparral country were taken with the sales manager and his wife. During that time, Gerry had begun talking to Charlene about his fantasy again, and he started looking at the couple's eleven-year-old daughter with predatory eyes. He remarked to Charlene that she resembled Sally Jo when she was younger.

"She would be just right," Gerry whispered to Charlene on one trip. "It would be so easy. She'd get right into the van with us."

"You're not going to do that, not to her," Charlene said firmly. "I won't let you."

It was one of the few times Charlene had drawn the line.

Summer came to the high desert. The snowline retreated up the slopes of the eastern wall of the Sierra Nevada until it lay in patches only on the highest peaks. Reno baked under a blazing sky in the afternoons.

Sunday, June 24, 1979, was Father's Day. Gerry rode with Charlene through the streets of Reno. They had just left the home of the sales manager and his family.

Gerry began talking again in that insane way of his about how easy it would be to entice the little girl into the van. Charlene talked him out of the idea by pointing out the very real danger of their personal connection with the family. But underneath her logical argument, Charlene was terrified. She knew it was happening again. Though Gerry never talked about rape and murder in so many words, she could see that he wanted to do it all over again. Anything, absolutely anything, would be better than letting Gerry kidnap her friend's little daughter.

"Baby, I want to do it again," he moaned. "But this time I want to do it right."

The Washoe County Fair was the biggest summer event in Reno for the majority of the city's residents whose lives seldom came into contact with chorus lines or crap tables. Gerry knew about the fair, and he suggested they go there. It should be a happy hunting ground, full of tender, slender girls with lean, tanned legs and blossoming bodies moving rhythmically in tight jeans — young girls with soft and unblemished complexions.

Fourteen-year-old Brenda Judd and thirteen-year-old Sandra Colley undoubtedly had been warned about men like Gerald Gallego. But they probably didn't really believe someone like him actually existed. Gerald Gallego was a shadow from another world. For kids like Brenda and Sandra, a guy like Gerry and the things he did to girls couldn't be real. That is, not until that Father's Day afternoon when Gerry and Charlene pulled up to the Washoe County Fair in their van with the foreboding vultures on the side.

Brenda and Sandra were among the happy crowd, enjoying the carefree celebration . . .

*       *       *

They had settled on a story for Charlene to tell the girls. She was working for the fair and needed someone to distribute advertising circulars. They would have to go to the van and wait until the circulars arrived.

Luck smiled on the first girl who caught Gerry's eye. She was a little charmer, just right for him, with a lovely, petite figure, honey blonde hair, pretty features. She really wanted the circular distributing job, too. On the way to the van, she told Charlene that her uncle was one of the people in charge of security at the fair and that she had to check with him and tell him what she would be doing.

Whatever else was running through Charlene's mind at the time, she did not want to get caught. Nieces of security officers of any rank were not on her list of candidates for Gerry's moribund harem. When the girl returned, Charlene

46

told her she had found someone else. The girl went away disappointed, never aware of her fortuitous luck.

A young man was walking from car to car in the parking lot, putting advertising leaflets under windshield wipers. Gerry removed some and gave them to Charlene, indicating she could use these to help in her sales pitch. As they entered the fairgrounds again, he pointed to a grassy mound not far from the entrance.

"I'll wait for you there," he said. "I'll be able to see you."

Charlene walked along the midway, a .38 caliber revolver Gerry had purchased for her heavy in her purse. What was she to do with it? She could not imagine shooting anyone. She knew Gerry was carrying a .44 caliber over-and-under derringer in the pocket of his jacket. She had no trouble imagining him shooting someone.

She strolled through the fairgrounds, through the waning sunlight, concentrating more intently on her task than she had in Sacramento's Country Club Plaza. There was more at stake in Reno. A little girl she knew, the daughter of a man she liked very much, might be the next victim if she failed to help Gerry satisfy his lewd and vicious appetite. Or so she reasoned.

Wandering through the crowd that was so oblivious to her mission, she found no one who would please Gerry. Still clutching the circulars, she walked back to the gate.

A moment or two later, they would have been safe. Brenda Judd and Sandra Colley almost reached the gate out of the fair when Charlene spotted them. She hurried over and made her prepared pitch. Charlene was persuasive, and she soon lured the two teen-agers into her snare.

Charlene called to Gerry, using the name of the sales manager instead, telling him they were going to take the leaflet distributing job. "I'm taking them back to the van to get more leaflets," she yelled.

Gerry nodded and followed at a distance. Charlene climbed into the van with the two girls.

And then he was standing beside her, holding a gun and licking his lips. Perhaps she handed him the .38 she had been

47

carrying. Later, she couldn't be sure. She was living in a strange world consisting of two dimensions — one in which she observed and the other in which she participated. Later, she would have a hard time distinguishing between the two. They had added a bed to the van, and Gerry told the girls to lie face down on the thin mattress that was covered by two blankets, one plaid and the other bright yellow. The girls obeyed. As they stared at the gun and the man who was holding it, the color drained from their faces. They trembled, and tears misted in their eyes. But they did what they were told, lying quietly on the blankets while Gerry bound them hand and foot.

One of the girls, the slender brunette with long hair that reached almost to her waist, vomited. Charlene saw the girl gasping and gagging and wanted to help her because she knew Gerry became angry when anyone was sick. A sour odor soon dominated the air in the van. Charlene, sitting in the back with the girls, reached out and patted the girl, telling her it would be all right, repeating it again and again while they rode out of the lot and toward Interstate 80.

Before they reached the highway, Gerry stopped the van in the parking lot of a building supply store, leaving Charlene to watch over the girls. She was back on the ice chest, still stroking the whimpering girl with the long hair and reassuring her. Charlene stayed in the van, never moving from her perch, never thinking of letting the girls out to safety.

Gerry returned after a short time, carrying a long-handled shovel with a golden-colored blade. He had also purchased a new hammer. Putting the tools into the back of the van, he climbed in behind the steering wheel.

Driving out of the parking lot, he turned east on the interstate and went through Sparks, then into the high, dry hills with their blanket of sagebrush. They went past the tiny hamlet of Mustang with its hump-backed shadows of wrecked automobiles and a collection of battered trailers on the hilltop. The single light punctuating this ugliness was the only clue that this was the site of one of the most notorious brothels in the world. Gerry smugly joked about men with sex drives and fat wallets waiting in line.

Charlene looked at the shovel with its golden blade and the hammer, still covered with transparent plastic wrapping. All the while, she kept stroking the head of the sick girl. "You'll be all right," she murmured. "Everything will be all right."

The brief, desert twilight had dropped over Washoe County as the van moved east on the highway. There was a sharp, clanging sound in the back of the van as it passed over a pothole in the road and the head of the hammer met the blade of the shovel.

The sight of the famed whorehouse apparently had awakened Gerry's own urges, because the van was only a few miles past Mustang when he had Charlene change seats with him. They traded places without stopping. Gerry, in the back with the girls, began giving orders to his new slaves.

"Get undressed. Take your clothes off."

Charlene could see in the rear-view mirror that the girls had stripped to their bras and panties and then stopped.

"Take everything off," Gerry ordered. "Take it all off."

When the girls were naked, he pushed them back down on the bed and out of Charlene's line of vision in the mirror. But she knew Gerry was untying them. He was even polite about it as he stared down at the girls and talked, either to himself or to Charlene, about their figures. She heard him remark how the one girl was so well-built.

It was never completely dark. A full moon rose over the rolling desert hills and saturated both the countryside and the van with its white light. Charlene could see enough to know that Gerry had mounted the girl whose figure he'd admired. Then, there were the unmistakable sounds of sex. Perhaps he took the other girl later, the one who had become sick. Charlene couldn't be sure.

Charlene knew the girls were crying. She could imagine the tears on their pretty, young faces with the fresh, unblemished skin and delicate coloring of youth.

The van rolled on, over the straight road with its sparse traffic and occasional sweeping curves, picking up speed as Charlene's throttle foot began to get heavy. Whatever Gerry was doing, he was not so preoccupied that he failed to complain in loud, angry tones.

"Slow down! Keep it at 55."

Charlene had a difficult time controlling the speed. The van seemed to have a mind of its own, wanting to go faster. Or maybe it was she wanting to get away from what was happening just a few feet behind her. On through the moonlit night they rode, maybe fifty miles further until they reached a lonely road with a gravel surface where Gerry told her to turn off and drive toward the hills.

Even on the gravel road, she drove too fast. First it was, "Hey, baby, what are you trying to do to us back here?" and when she yelled back at him, he replied with a venomous curse in her ear, "You dumb bitch!"

He took over the driving. The van moved slower then, over the moon-washed road past clusters of chaparral, toward an area where they had once camped with another couple. Charlene thought of the sales manager's daughter, who would have been naked in the van, too, if Gerry had his way.

Her mind was numb. She was living in a nightmare, but this time she knew it was real. This was no dream, no joke, and there would be no surprise happy ending. The two girls, the two pretty teen-agers who had been having so much fun at the county fair, would be led off into the darkness and never be seen alive again. Charlene, who felt protective toward the girl with long hair, was afraid for her. She was also frightened for herself because she had dared to shout back at Gerry.

They drove to where the hills rose sharply away from the little valley with its cover of scrawny piñons and juniper to a place where a small stream tumbled down the slope and slashed a ragged wash through the brush. Then she and the girl with the long hair were alone. Gerry was gone with the other girl, the one for whom Charlene had no feelings. He had stopped the van and walked off into the night with her, taking the shovel with its gilded blade and the new hammer with him.

Charlene wondered if she would hear the popping sound again, but this time there was no noise at all. She waited in the dark. The girl with the long hair huddled, still nude, at her feet. Charlene stroked the girl's hair and spoke soothingly to her. "Everything will be all right. Everything will be fine."

The girl was crying softly, ever so softly. She looked up at Charlene now and then with eyes that were filled with a mixture of fear and anger. It was as if the teen-ager was silently beseeching, *How could you have let this happen?*

Charlene reached down and smoothed her mussed hair. "It's okay, honey. It'll be all right."

Maybe she meant it. Charlene felt a strange attachment for the girl and wanted to help her. But before she could formulate a thought, maybe even a plan, Gerry was back.

Charlene had already dismissed the first girl, the one with the body that Gerry liked so much, from her mind. She didn't matter. But the girl with the long hair did. Charlene reached down and could feel the girl's damp cheeks.

Gerry looked at the girl at Charlene's feet and said harshly, "Come on. You're next."

"No," Charlene objected. The sternness in her voice surprised her. "I don't want you to take her." Charlene wanted to touch the girl again, to tell her it would be all right.

But then Gerry was snarling at her. "You're fucking everything up, you bitch!"

He grabbed Charlene, pinning her arms to her sides, then shoved her back against the wall of the van. His face was livid with rage.

"If you don't shut the fuck up I'm going to make you do it!"

"I don't want you to take her." Charlene's protest was weaker this time. "*Please*, Gerry." She could see the girl's eyes. She was still crying softly, but her eyes reflected anger now. The girl was clearly outraged at the indignity she had endured and at the fate she must have known awaited her.

Charlene watched numbly as Gerry dragged the girl out of the van and pulled her into the darkness. Charlene felt as though he was taking her, too.

When he returned, alone, he was carrying the hammer and shovel.

Charlene looked at him and hated him. For the first time in her life, she despised Gerald Gallego. She stared at him, anger filling her pale blue eyes. Then she asked the question she knew was hardly necessary. But she needed to know.

"Did you kill her?"

"Yeah, I killed her. I'll kill you, too."

It was now a possibility she could not overlook. She knew he *could* kill her if he thought about it long enough. She stood in the moonlight, hating the sight of him, and afraid.

Gerry put the shovel away and climbed behind the wheel. Charlene got into the passenger's seat. She still felt a bond with the doomed girl with the long hair. She ignored Gerry and stared out the window.

The van grumbled to life and moved back over the bumpy road to the highway. Gerry made a remark about running out of hammers. The hammer he'd purchased in Sparks was sitting on the floor of the van beneath his legs, right next to the console. Charlene noticed that it had a blue rubber handle. It was time to get rid of it, she thought. The hammer should have been thrown from the window of the van. Amazingly, Gerry was worried about running out of hammers.

Gerry drove through the night until the lights of a service station tore through the darkness. He pulled off the road and stopped beside the pumps to purchase gas. Charlene was asleep by then. She woke up when she heard the service station attendant shouting, and she looked out the window to see him gesturing to Gerry. When Gerry returned to the van, she asked him what was wrong.

"The guy was ripped off," Gerry said. "Somebody held him up. Now get out of my face." He was angry and sour again. He told her to get into the back of the van and lie down.

Charlene did as she was told, crawling over the console and into the rear of the van, then stretching out on the bed. Asleep just moments before, she was now wide awake and frozen with fear.

Stench filled her nostrils. She could distinguish the rancid odor of old vomit as it blended with the sickening-sweet smell of stale sex — an offensive olfactory cocktail which repelled and disgusted her. She pushed the pillowcase away. It was damp in spots. As she did, she became painfully aware of the situation she was in. Here she was lying on a bed which had recently been occupied by two girls who had been so alive and innocent and unsuspecting. Girls who were now dead. And now she was the one on that bed in the van driven by their killer. The odor disgusted her, nauseated her, but her fear of the man at the wheel was stronger than either. She stayed on the bed, worrying. Despite her terror for her life she also experienced a different kind of fear. She was afraid that she was no longer attractive to Gerry, that he'd lost interest in her. Even if he didn't kill her, she was afraid he would dump her.

For miles, as the van rolled back through the dark hills under a pale moon which had rushed across the night sky and was nearing the western horizon, she stayed motionless, wide awake and terrified.

"Get back up here!" he finally ordered.

Charlene couldn't wait to obey. Sitting back in the passenger's seat beside Gerry, free of the smell, no longer lying in the victims' bed, and next to her master, she managed to go to sleep again. When she awoke, she saw a brightly illuminated highway sign suspended high over a Reno freeway. She knew they were near home.

When they reached their apartment, they both fell into bed. Gerry was still angry. Before too long, he kicked her out of the bed. "You're too goddamned skinny," he complained.

# The Father

*I didn't want to stay with one woman long, because there was always new pleasures to be found. One night while I was drinking heavy, I decided to go and steal my stepfather's car. Later, my stepfather and mom accused me of taking the car, but I maintained my innocence. They asked me if I would be willing to tell the police what I had told them. When confronted with the police, they were going to lock me up, so I broke and ran and made good my escape. I went to Salt Lake City to live with my older sister but after awhile I came back to California to see my girlfriend. While I was away, a warrant had been issued for my arrest. I was hitchhiking over to my girlfriend's when I saw these plainclothes men drive up. They recognized me at once, and I started to run. One of the cops got out of the car and fired three shots at me. None of the shots hit me, and again I made good my escape. I went to my girlfriend's and asked her if she wanted to live with me in Salt Lake City. She said yes, and at once began to pack her things. It was then a knock sounded at the door, and parked outside was three cars and seven cops. I ran and hid in her closet, and the cops searched the house from all corners and were unable to find me. When the cops were finally giving up in disgust, one of the wise cops decided to take another look in the closet where I was hiding. They finally found me. But it took all seven of those cops to put the cuffs on me. It was then I vowed vengeance. I swore I would kill the next cop that ever tried to arrest me.*

From the death row statement of Gerald Albert Gallego
Mississippi State Prison
Jackson, Mississippi

# Six

*Lt. Biondi — Homicide*

When Brenda Judd and Sandra Colley were snared by Charlene Williams, they had been waiting for an older sister who was scheduled to meet them near the entrance to the Washoe County Fair. The sister arrived shortly after the girls were kidnapped, waited for them, then began hunting through the crowded fairgrounds, thinking they were having so much fun they'd forgotten to watch the time.

Later that day, she reported the girls missing to the Reno Police Department. The possibility of a runaway situation was discussed. This seemed remote. Neither girl had any severe personal problems. They were healthy, well-behaved, and reasonably sensible for their ages. According to their friends, neither was experimenting with drugs or liquor. There had never been any indication that either girl was unhappy at home.

Both girls lived in broken homes, but they were the daughters of parents who, however incompatible, were well adjusted to their situation. There was nothing about their home lives to drive them away.

Reno police combed the city while searching for the missing teen-agers. They interviewed scores of employees and visitors to the fairgrounds and found the usual number of people who were sure they had seen Brenda and Sandra. For instance, several people claimed to have seen two girls preparing to run away with the carnival that provided games and thrill rides for the midway. Their stories were so detailed and persistent that Reno police followed the trail of the carnival to Salt Lake City where they discovered the yarn was true. Two other Reno girls *had* run away with the carnival. But, of course, they were not Brenda Judd and Sandra Colley.

As the hunt persisted and the trail cooled, Reno police investigators followed leads into southern California and north into Oregon and Washington. Frequently, they located runaways, but not Brenda or Sandra.

Never was the possibility of kidnapping or murder mentioned to the families of the two girls. And neither family gave up hope of seeing their daughter alive again. One group of relatives, following a specious tip, spent weeks in the Lake Tahoe area, checking resort after resort. Sightings of the two girls were reported all over the West. But Brenda Judd and Sandra Colley were never found.

In Sacramento, we continued to work on the Vaught-Scheffler murders. Hot pursuit cooled, as it always will when a case gets old and the trail worn and trampled. My system of immediately putting as many detectives as possible on the case and not letting up until the mystery is cleared did not work in the case of Kippi Vaught and Rhonda Scheffler.

But, unlike the Reno Police Department, we knew Rhonda and Kippi had been murdered. And we had a lead, one that looked very good for a while. Person after person claimed to have seen the two girls ride away with the two black men in the maroon car. Everyone concerned with the investigation became convinced that was what happened.

We found another man who had been with them at the mall. He told us about meeting Rhonda and Kippi there, waiting while they entered a store and shopped for shoes and then going with them to another store to buy three cans of motor oil. He told us he had asked them for a ride across town and that Rhonda had said she couldn't take him because she needed to pick up her husband at work. The time, he said, was shortly before 4:30 in the afternoon. It coincided almost exactly with the time that Rhonda and Kippi had been seen entering the maroon car.

When we located the counselor who owned the maroon Firebird, we advised him of his Miranda rights, but we never found solid enough evidence to charge him. Also, there was that inconclusive polygraph test. As the investigation progressed, I became increasingly convinced that the guy with the maroon car had *not* committed the murders.

That, too, is the job of a homicide investigator. I have always believed we must not only be able to find the guilty but also to establish an innocent person's lack of guilt.

In late June of 1979, when Brenda Judd and Sandra Colley were kidnapped and murdered in Nevada, we were still following leads in the Vaught-Scheffler investigation, giving it all the time our work load would allow. Homicides are not committed on a set schedule. They are not distributed evenly over a period of time. They come in bunches, at times, causing our small squad to strain under the work load. Then there are periods between these bursts of activity when we have time to go over the stubborn mysteries which are still unsolved. But we continue to follow leads, and sometimes a crack begins to show in the puzzle's protective shield.

We gave the Vaught-Scheffler case every bit of time we could between other, more recent homicide cases. But to no avail. At times, all our accumulated experience, skill, and scientific and technical knowledge seem useless until we get that first break.

Twenty long months after the killings of Kippi Vaught and Rhonda Scheffler, I began to hope for Lady Luck to stop holding hands with their killer or killers long enough so that we could get the break we so desperately needed.

# Seven

Charlene cleaned the van when they returned to Reno. She washed the bedding and resumed her life with Gerald Gallego. The hatred she had felt for him that night beside the little spring northeast of Lovelock still flared occasionally, though less often now. ·

Life changed for the two of them. Gerry had never been a sensitive lover, always a demanding one. Now, his level of cruelty had increased to the point where she wanted to cower from his touch. In his mind, it was her womanly duty to provide him with any sexual activity he desired, from masturbation to fellatio to sodomy. Sex was for him alone. And if it hurt or disgusted her, well, that was her problem. At the same time, Charlene's feelings toward the sales manager kept growing. She saw him often, too often, as it turned out. Eventually, Gerry saw them driving together in the van. He was furious, causing an awful scene. After that, Charlene decided it just wasn't worth Gerry's ire, so she cooled her friendship with the man before it was consummated.

In early July, 1979, Gerry found a new job driving a delivery truck for a soft drink company in Reno. Later that month, he went to a sporting goods store and bought a .357 magnum Colt Python, a formidable handgun. He lost his job again, but he still seemed to have money. Many nights he was gone, always carrying the little over-and-under derringer with him. Gerry told Charlene he spent his time playing cards, and he always returned with a pile of money. And yet, whenever Charlene went gambling with Gerry he'd lose. Charlene never tried to add up the possibilities of what Gerry might really be doing on his nights out with the short-barreled, high-caliber weapon.

Now flush with his mysterious money, he taunted Charlene that she was not earning enough, not being paid what she was worth. Tired of hearing his complaints, she quit her job with the meat company in late September. By then, they had moved to an apartment in another area of Reno. Still impotent, Gerry stopped wanting to sleep in the master bedroom, preferring the smaller front bedroom with twin beds. Sometimes they shared the same bed, cuddling closely together like two frightened puppies. But most nights they slept separately.

She hated the front bedroom. It was dark in there, always too dark, and she had grown to fear the darkness. One night when Gerry was out, she was lying alone on one of the twin beds. The shadows closed around her, a tight little tomb, and suddenly, inexplicably, she was absolutely terrified. She couldn't move. Fearful of going downstairs or into the bedroom or anyplace else, she stayed in the bed, lying very still, afraid to let a muscle twitch, held there by the unyielding hand of unseen terror.

A short time later, they moved back to California, renting a duplex unit in a fairly new, middle-class area of Sacramento. Woodhollow Drive was a pleasant neighborhood of carefully manicured lawns and healthy young trees.

Charlene registered with the meat cutters union and worked fairly steadily, mostly for the large, locally owned supermarket chain which had first enticed her father to Sacramento years earlier.

Gerry and Charlene lived as Mr. and Mrs. Stephen Feil and quickly became friendly with the couple living in the next apartment. The young man admired Gerry's collection of guns which now included an AR-15 rifle and a gleaming, chrome .38, in addition to the over-and-under derringer and .357 magnum.

Gerry applied for a California driver's license as Stephen Feil. A few weeks later, Charlene accepted a job which involved traveling with a food distributing firm. Among the cities she visited regularly were Reno and Winnemucca, a town far beyond Lovelock on Interstate 80.

Charlene's new position was a long step toward the realization of her dream to make her own way in the business world. At twenty-one, she was the only woman on the sales staff, but she didn't mind. As a youngster, she'd watched her father make his way up the corporate ladder, and she felt comfortable attempting to do the same thing. She had always felt comfortable in a man's world.

As a schoolgirl, Charlene had been bashful with her schoolmates. She thought of herself as a funny little kid with pigtails and braces on her teeth. Introduced to the violin in the fourth grade, she began to find herself. Pleased by his daughter's obvious talent, Chuck Williams bought her a violin to fit her size. Charlene and her instrument became inseparable, and she began to talk about attending the Juilliard School of Music. But her mother worried about Charlene's passion for music. It was nice for a young lady to be able to play an instrument, but the life of a professional musician was not something she wanted for her daughter.

Shy or not, Charlene's intelligence took her to the top in school, and in the sixth grade she was placed in a class for the mentally gifted. Before her introduction to sex, drugs, and alcohol, she had been a student leader who was almost overwhelmed by extracurricular activities. She played in the school orchestra and handled various behind-the-scenes responsibilities, including acting as student director for the school's dramatic productions.

Now entering her third decade of life, Charlene believed her new job would finally give her the opportunity to use those leadership skills she'd discovered early in life.

Through October and November, 1979, Gerry worked as a driver for a valley trucking company, working a route which took him to the San Francisco Bay Area, sometimes on overnight trips. With a job again, his impotency disappeared, and once again he was the insatiable lover Charlene had known during the beginning of their relationship. He held on to this job for almost three months.

It was almost Christmas, December 21, 1979, when Gerry went to work as a bartender at a North Sacramento tavern. For reasons he never explained to Charlene, he always introduced her as his girlfriend when she visited him at the club. Patrons who knew they were married joked among themselves about the arrangement. They knew what Charlene did not know — that Gerry was dating some of the women customers — though this certainly would not have surprised her.

Gerry was an attentive bartender, and he developed a following at the club. His knowledge of the bartender's bible was sufficient to satisfy the plebeian tastes of his customers. He felt powerful and comfortable behind the bar. Men liked his manly airs, and a number of women were attracted to his rugged looks and macho ways.

Evelyn Smith, blonde, blue-eyed, slender, and broke, walked into the bar one February evening in 1980. A little depressed, she was anxious to strike up a conversation with the muscular bartender working behind the plank. As they chatted, she put away enough drinks to make her feel woozy. When he locked up the place at two o'clock in the morning, Gerry asked Evelyn to have breakfast with him at an all-night diner. She accepted. Over coffee and eggs, he told her he was divorced. Would she like to take a ride with him after the meal? She said sure, why not?

She rode around with him in the Olds until four o'clock in the morning, when he dropped her off at the home of her parents, where she was living temporarily. He suggested they meet again. She said yes.

They met again for breakfast and rode off into the dark countryside where they made love in the back seat of Charlene's Oldsmobile. The relationship bloomed into a passionate, almost nightly affair. He told her he loved her and she thought she loved him. Gerry's sex drive and her attraction to him produced a nonstop amorous appetite in each of them. When they were together, they made love as much as five times a night, registering at motels scattered throughout northern California.

Evelyn's family did not share her feelings for Gerry. When he was introduced to them, an instant mutual dislike and distrust developed. She moved out of her parents' home into one motel and then another, with Gerry always paying the rent.

Gerry had not given up Charlene. He felt an attachment of his own to the woman with whom he had shared so much. Somewhere he found the strength to spend part of most nights with Evelyn, then get up and go home. Evelyn knew that meant he was married, but it didn't matter. She was sure the time would come when he'd leave his wife. Then Evelyn would have Gerry all to herself.

Charlene was not always home to welcome her philandering husband, and their frequent separations may have been one reason why she was enjoying her life more. Her new job took her over a wide area. She traveled north as far as Medford, Oregon, and east to Winnemucca, Nevada, with stops in Reno. The drive from Reno to Winnemucca was long and tiresome through the high desert, with only a few scattered small towns breaking up the endless sagebrush scenery. One of these towns was Lovelock, the county seat of Pershing County, huddled next to Interstate 80 where it skirts the Humboldt Sink and the valley around it. Charlene never thought much about Lovelock except that the word was out about the danger of speed traps in that area.

Fifty miles northeast of Lovelock, long before she reached Winnemucca, she passed the gravel road leading to the hills and the small stream where two teen-age lives had abruptly ended.

Charlene pushed the gas pedal to the floor, not worrying about a speeding ticket. Trying to keep her mind on her job and what she would be doing in Winnemucca, she tried not to remember the girl with the long hair.

*     *     *

There was never any predicting of Gerry's moods. Despite his passionate affair with Evelyn Smith — which Charlene still knew nothing about — he began talking again to his wife about his fantasies. The urge was developing once more and it was one he would not ignore. The circumstances of his fantasy life had changed so subtly that not even Charlene's keen mind caught the shift. For the first time, he wanted his love slaves even when he was employed and potent. He had become a walking sexual time bomb, and Charlene was not sure when he'd next go off.

One spring evening in 1980, he and Charlene went to the club where Gerry worked. For the first hour or so, they got along fine. Then, for no apparent reason, his disposition changed. He behaved so outrageously that Charlene forgot her guilt and her fears, and after they left the bar, she jumped out of the car when he stopped for a traffic signal. When he caught her, she told him she just couldn't live with him anymore. When the storm passed, she calmed, outwardly at least, and they went home together. But their relationship was changing rapidly. Gerry would find fault with everything she did. Charlene wondered if there was another woman and found herself almost hoping there was. It would take some of the pressure off her.

On March 26th, Charlene applied for a .25 caliber Beretta automatic pistol at a Sacramento sporting goods store. It was something Gerry had asked her to do for him, and it was always easier to do what he said than to argue with him.

On April 14th, Charlene picked up the Beretta. She bought some ammunition the same day at another store and delivered it and the gun to the bar where Gerry was working. On the way home, she had a fender bender. Neither car nor driver was hurt, but Charlene reflected that things were beginning to go bad. Was their luck running out?

By April 24th, 1980, Gerry was ready to fulfill another fantasy. He made plans with Charlene and made sure the shovel and a new hammer were in the van. Then they drove to Tower Records, almost across the street from the Country

Club Plaza where Rhonda Scheffler and Kippi Vaught were kidnapped a year and a half earlier.

"It's too early," Charlene told Gerry when he was disappointed by the sparse foot traffic at the record store, a favorite gathering place for teen-agers. "Everybody is still in school."

"Just find a girl!" he exploded. "You're not being paid to think."

He told her it might be best if they went to Country Club again. Charlene shrank from the idea. She did *not* want to go back there. He told her to think of some place where she could find a girl. The incongruity didn't escape Charlene. A moment earlier, he'd told her she wasn't being paid to think. Now he was telling her to do just that. Her heart wasn't in this. She wanted him to leave her alone. She was sick of it all.

They drove away from Tower Records. Awakening from her dark thoughts, Charlene noticed that they were approaching a long white structure with red and yellow flags and a big red sign on top.

Sunrise Mall opened before them, and they parked the van near a large department store and began walking. They passed an ice cream restaurant, then another department store, and down the row of smaller shops. They paused beside a fountain. Gerry stopped and sat down. There were people in the mall, a lot of people. He looked at Charlene.

"Go to it," he said sharply.

*Go to it?* She was back in that other world, watching herself wander numbly through the mall, deadly and depressed, an angel of death. It was happening all over again. There was nothing she could do about it. She had convinced herself of that. A security guard, armed and muscular, roamed through the center. A lone patrol car eased through the parking lot and back to the street. Charlene ignored them. She told herself that no one could help her or the girls she was required to find for Gerry's Stygian fantasy.

The two girls were standing near the window of a department store with shopping bags in their hands. One of them was slim with straight, dark hair. The other was a slender blonde. Each of them resembled Charlene!

Charlene went about her task with automated efficiency. She befriended them, asking them what they did and how they spent their free time. Then she started strolling along with them, past the fountain and past Gerry, who watched until they were a safe distance away. Then he followed.

\*    \*    \*

There had been tears on each of the previous occasions when the girls realized what was happening to them. This time it was different. Charlene could feel the difference.

Gerry entered the van, reached for the .357 magnum in the console, and said softly, "You girls are being kidnapped." The brunette became very quiet. She was now leaning against the side of the van as though waiting for the next development. She watched and listened but talked very little.

The blonde asked questions. She seemed curious, almost eager. It seemed to Charlene that the girl was thinking of this in terms of a new adventure. *How right she was*, Charlene reflected. It would be the biggest adventure of her life. And the last.

Gerry, gun in hand, sat down and chatted with them. He asked the girls about themselves, what they did and where they came from. The blonde seemed to enjoy the questioning and talked animatedly as if she'd just found a new friend.

Charlene, struggling in that dual world where she resided through these episodes, had trouble focusing. She was trying to absorb the curious situation. Why was Gerry talking to the girl like an old friend? Then it hit her. He was systematically and deliberately finding out all the things he needed to know.

The blonde was visiting her friend, the brunette. The blonde had run away from home. Her parents lived in Nevada and would not miss her right away. The girls were scheduled to meet the brunette's mother that afternoon, but they'd missed such appointments in the past. Their failure to appear this afternoon would not cause any immediate concern.

Even with her knowledge of what the inevitable macabre ending would be to this adventure, Charlene allowed herself the luxury of snobbery. These girls, she thought smugly, were from "the other side of the tracks" — certainly not the type of kids she'd grown up with.

Then the formalities ended and Gerry got down to business. He had them lie down side by side on the bed and bound them. He drove toward the interstate, stopping long enough on the way to hop into a telephone booth and call the club to say he was sick and would not be at work.

He found a ramp and drove onto the highway, moving east toward the Sierra Nevada and Reno. The girls both stayed quiet now, lying on the moribund cradle exactly where Brenda Judd and Sandra Colley had rested before embarking on a premature departure into eternity.

They passed Baxter and a familiar sign pointing the way to a frontage road. Charlene formed a mental picture of the first two girls who had made that trip with them. Gerry maneuvered the van up the steep highway and through the tall pines, traveling an even 55 miles an hour.

She glanced back at the two girls on the bed — doomed children, too young, too innocent, too confident to be afraid. Charlene knew the day would end in death for two more girls. They would be eliminated, and then somehow she and Gerry would go on with their life together.

Baxter, a hamlet clinging to a pine-studded mountain, appeared and then disappeared. This was close to where it all began, Charlene realized. And since then, it had happened again. And now again. And who knew how many more times? Wasn't there any way to stop it? Wasn't there any way out? She could think of none.

Gerry, behind the wheel, was tripping on down the road happy as he could be, the radio blasting country-western hits that, Charlene knew, made him feel like a cowboy stud. He was acting as though this were a perfectly normal way to spend an afternoon. But she knew it was sick, terribly sick. The morbid reality of the situation overwhelmed her thoughts. It was happening all over again!

The van moved up the Sierra Nevada to where the afternoon sun painted the granite spires pink and carnelian. Patches of snow at the roadside became an icy wall that hemmed in the broad, twisting byway. The warmth of the valley was gone, replaced by the chilly bite of springtime in the Sierra.

Over Donner Summit they rolled, where diehard skiers warmed themselves with hot-buttered rums in the bar at Soda Springs. Then down the steep east wall of the Sierra where the long shadows of the mountains blotted out the afternoon sun and it was cold, cold, cold. Charlene shivered as she sat and watched the girl with the eyelet blouse who must have been freezing as the frosted air swept through the pattern of perforations in her garment. But the girl didn't complain.

Beyond Donner Lake, Interstate 80 rolled east toward Reno, following the bank of the Truckee River, swollen and murky with the runoff from the snow-capped mountains. The road dropped, then ascended slightly, cutting through a hill at the end of a mountain valley. Reno sprawled below them, gilded, shining, the city of sin, wearing jewels of sapphire and ruby neon as evening approached and sparkling in places where windows in tall buildings caught the dying rays of a setting sun.

They rode on, through the gathering darkness into a narrow canyon that followed the river as it rolled and riffled toward the thirsty sands which would drink and swallow the snow-born torrent when it reached Pyramid Lake.

Ninety miles northeast of Reno, they reached Lovelock and stopped at a white stucco service station.

"They'll be all right," Gerry told Charlene when she asked if he wanted her in the back to watch the girls.

Then, talking to all three of them, or so it seemed, he said: "I know you're not going to do anything stupid like yell or make noises."

He left the van to buy gas. The service station attendant had no reason to be suspicious. Nothing ever happened in Lovelock, other than a fatal accident on the highway now and then. Gerry filled the van with gas and then drove out of the city about fifteen miles until he reached the Oreana turnoff. He took the turnoff straight east, toward the hills along a road Charlene recognized immediately because they had been camping there before with another couple.

Almost five miles along the road, as it reached the hills, a stand of cottonwood, rare in that part of Nevada, rises beside the bed of a lively little stream which flows down the hills to the valley floor and meets the Humboldt River. The stream bed is broad and lined with brush, but the water withdraws to its center when the winter runoff is over.

It is a beautiful little oasis, as Nevada scenery goes, and popular with the people of Pershing County as a picnic area on warm summer weekends. But on chilly weekday nights in the springtime, it is lonely and deserted.

Gerry parked the van, and when he did, Charlene got out and walked off by herself in the deep twilight. She hated the dark ever since that night in Baxter and Sloughhouse off the Old Jackson Road. But she was more afraid of hearing and seeing what was going to happen in the van than she was of the enveloping darkness.

After a time, Gerry called her back to the van.

The calm which had prevailed inside the van earlier had long since departed. The girls looked at her with shocked, terrified, reproachful eyes. Gerry had finished with them and he'd already retied their hands. He took out the shovel and went off into the hills, telling Charlene to watch the girls.

She sat in the cab, frightened as she had never been before. The interior of the van was dark, ominously so, and she could hear the girls breathing right behind her. One girl was desperately drawing the thin air of the high desert in and out of her lungs as if she couldn't catch her breath. Charlene turned up the radio to blot out their sounds. The music didn't help Charlene. The girls were still back there, still breathing, and she was still frightened. She wanted Gerry to hurry up and come back. He would, of course, come back to lead the girls to the graves he was digging. It was, Charlene thought wryly, unusually thoughtful of him to dig the graves ahead of time so they wouldn't have to watch.

When Gerry returned to the van, he asked Charlene to hand him the hammer. It was in the cabinet. To get it, either he or she would have to reach across the girls.

Charlene didn't move a muscle.

He told her to go ahead and do it. She shrank away, telling him he had promised her she would never have to do any of it. She no longer wanted to be the girl with heart. She wanted no part of it.

Gerry told her to forget it and made another offer. "Do you want them?" he asked.

*He's sick*, Charlene thought again. Terribly, terribly sick. She told him she didn't want the girls. Not in the way he meant.

"I feel bad because you never get anything out of these things," he said.

*I don't want anything out of it*, she was thinking. *I don't want the girls. I don't want you. I don't want anything.*

Gallego went to the rear of the van and pulled one of the girls out. He dragged her by the feet, over the top of the other girl, talking all the time.

"Come on over the top of your friend here. Move on over. Now move!"

Gallego slipped off into the shadows carrying the hammer and leading the girl he had just dragged from the van. A short time later, he returned for the second girl. Over the blaring radio, Charlene could hear the van doors slam as Gerry took the girl away, into the darkness toward the stream bed carved by the little creek. The hammer was still in his hand. He was not gone long. When he returned, the hammer was sticky with blood. He wanted Charlene to go with him to look at the graves.

Charlene didn't want to look at the graves. It was bad enough knowing they were there. But Gerry insisted, and she began to think there might be a third grave out in the darkness. A special grave for her.

Gerry led her to the dry area where the stream had narrowed as the winter runoff slowed. The soil was softened there and the digging had been easy.

There was no third grave. Just two long mounds in the armpit of the stream bed where the soft earth had been freshly turned.

A light breeze rustled the branches of the cottonwoods, and for one moment, one terrifying moment, it sounded like breathing.

Charlene trembled as she stood in the darkness. She remembered how she had felt when she was a little girl walking through a cemetery. She was always so cold, so very cold.

She hadn't wanted to see the graves. She didn't want to be near them. But Gerry was proud of his work. He wanted someone to see how well he had done. Finally, they went back to the van.

As they approached Interstate 80, Charlene threw the hammer out the window.

# Eight

*Lt. Biondi — Homicide*

Stacy Ann Redican, the blonde, and Karen Twiggs, the brunette, misinformed Gerald Gallego when they told him they would not be missed when they failed to keep an appointment with Karen's mother.

At Sacramento's Sunrise Mall, Mary Ann Twiggs had what she later described as a "mother's gut feeling" that her daughter was in danger when she and her friend failed to show up that afternoon. Later that night, Mrs. Twiggs went to the Sacramento Police Department and reported the girls' disappearance.

When she told the police about Stacy's history of running away, the authorities theorized she had returned to her old habits and taken her friend Karen with her. In fact, her latest leaving home had been the catalyst that brought Stacy to the Twiggs household. It was reasonable to believe she had taken off one more time, this time with her friend Karen as a companion.

A search for the two "runaway" girls was launched. Stacy's pattern in the past had been to call home and assure her parents she was unharmed and healthy. Almost everyone thought she would soon make another such call. Everyone except Mrs. Twiggs, that is, who felt a strong sense of foreboding.

When neither Karen nor Stacy called, Mrs. Twiggs was even more certain something had happened to them. Karen had never run away and was a conscientious and reliable member of a single-parent family.

Stacy Ann Redican was a native of Nevada. She had attended two years of high school in Reno, where she and Karen had been classmates and close friends. In 1979, when Karen and her mother moved away, an unhappy Stacy appeared a few days later at the Twiggs' new home in Sacramento. Arrangements were made for Stacy to live with them.

Within days, bulletins were dispatched by the Sacramento Police Department, and posters bearing photographs of the missing girls were distributed throughout the area. Still, the prevailing opinion of the authorities was that the two girls, both seventeen, were runaways.

As usual, there were reports that the girls had been seen in at least three states. The ugly truth, however, was uncovered by a mongrel dog belonging to a family picnicking in a grove of cottonwoods outside of Lovelock.

Long before the dog wandered into the brush which protected the stream bed, the family had noticed an unpleasant odor. The stench had cast a pall over the otherwise happy gathering, and one of the older members of the group had suggested it was the odor of death.

When the dog finally followed the malodorous air, his growls and barks drew one of the children to his side. The child's frightened calls summoned the rest of the family. They stopped abruptly at the edge of the little creek. It was a shocked and frightened group of adults and children that stared at the grisly sight before them. The unmistakable form of a human hand attached to an arm jutted out of the damp sand.

When they recovered from the shock of their discovery, the picnickers immediately packed their belongings and raced to the nearest telephone to call the Lovelock Police Department.

The shallow graves proudly prepared by Gerald Gallego had been easily violated by the lean and hungry coyotes who roam the back country of Nevada. The local police chief called Kay McIntosh, the Sheriff of Pershing County, who had the bodies transported to Reno where they were given an autopsy the next day. The medical examiner reported the bodies to be those of two young women who had been bludgeoned to death.

An account of the grim discovery in the hills northeast of Lovelock was published in the *Reno Gazette* and *Nevada Journal* and broadcast by Nevada radio and television stations. More than a week passed before Stacy Redican's mother, apprehensive, frightened, and praying that her hunch was wrong, added up the probabilities and came to the conclusion that one of the dead girls found near Lovelock might be her daughter. She took Stacy's dental charts to the Washoe County Sheriff's Department.

The sheriff's deputies called Tom Moots, an investigator for the Nevada Bureau of Investigation. Moots was one of a handful of investigators employed, whenever necessary, by the State of Nevada as sort of a traveling detective agency that is detailed to help law enforcement agencies in the state's large but sparsely populated counties.

Moots talked to Stacy's dentist in Reno and discovered that another dentist in the same building handled the dental work for Karen Twiggs. The investigator asked the dentists to compare the dental charts of the two girls with the medical examiner's findings. It didn't take the dentists long to report that their two patients were the murder victims.

Moots immediately began a detailed background investigation of Stacy and Karen. Hoping to find the key to the murders among the people who had known the two young women best, he talked to their friends, acquaintances, and relatives in Reno. When nothing developed in Nevada, he spent several weeks in Sacramento and its suburbs, interviewing Karen's mother and friends and every merchant in the Sunrise Mall. Moots also hunted down as many people as possible who had been shopping at the mall the day the girls disappeared.

In a way, and from my viewpoint as a homicide investigator, Moots was lucky in what he *didn't* find. Even though there were no clues as to why Karen and Stacy were kidnapped and murdered in a lonely Nevada desert canyon, there were also no persistent tips and misleading statements by witnesses which could have led Moots in the wrong direction, as in what happened in our investigation of the Vaught/Scheffler murders.

\*     \*     \*

Six young women had now been murdered, all of them in their teens. Gallego's fantasies had been unleashed, and with them his appetite for murder. He appeared to have discovered the ultimate climax for his sexual encounters. Death. Now his pattern was about to change.

# The Father

*I was examined by two psychiatrists. One believed me to be criminally insane, the other had hopes I would make the grade. After much deliberation, my parole officer decided to give me another chance . . . I killed a man because he made me sore. I killed him with my fists. I didn't think I had that much power in my punches. I took his money, put his body in the trunk of the car, and proceeded to dump his body in an oil sump where I knew they would never find him. I got rid of his car by selling it in Tijuana, Mexico, for $250.*

From the death row statement of Gerald Albert Gallego
Mississippi State Prison
Jackson, Mississippi, 1954

# Nine

When Charlene threw the hammer out the window of the van, she handled it the way she would have a dead rat. The hammer offended her and she didn't want to touch it, even though Gerry had wiped it clean with paper towels.

The van rolled on, toward Winnemucca, because Charlene had a business appointment there. During the ride, Gerry asked her to empty the girls' purses and lay everything she found on the floor in front of the console. After taking inventory, he pulled over at a rest stop and threw everything he thought was incriminating into a garbage can.

They spent the night at a roadside campground outside Winnemucca. Charlene wiped down the entire van while Gerry directed her efforts.

In the morning, she put on clean clothes, and they drove to town so she could call on her account. When her business call was concluded, she went to buy new clothes for Gerry. He needed new shoes, trousers, a shirt and jacket. Almost everything he wore the previous night had been stained with blood.

The next day, they headed back toward Sacramento. On the way they checked into a hotel at Lake Tahoe, near the crystal waters of one of the world's most beautiful lakes. But they stayed away from the glittering casinos. Gerry explained there was no point in playing a game which could not be rigged.

Back in Sacramento, they saw nothing in the newspapers about the disappearance of two teen-agers from Sunrise Mall, and they resumed their lives. Charlene continued to travel for the food distributor. Gerry turned his attention to wandering, often alone, along the streams above Grass Valley and Nevada City in California's Mother Lode country, looking for gold.

On June 1st, despite the rift which was growing between Gerry and her, they were married again as Mr. and Mrs. Stephen Feil. They had been sitting at the Red Dog Diggings near Grass Valley with a couple of friends from Sacramento talking about a proposed rafting trip. Someone in the group, not knowing that Gerry and Charlene Gallego were already married, suggested that Stephen Feil and his girlfriend should get married because they seemed so right for each other.

Gerry and Charlene thought it sounded like fun, so they drove back to Sacramento, packed, and headed over the mountains to Reno where they were married that day as Stephen and Charlene Feil in a picturesque little chapel.

They decided to take a short vacation, a sort of delayed honeymoon. They drove past Weed, where Mt. Shasta, monolithic giant of the Cascades, towered more than 14,000 feet above sea level, and on through the high, shallow pasture lands between there and Medford, Oregon, picking up a pair of hitchhikers along the way.

At Klamath Falls, they turned west toward the coast, then north, dropping their passengers at Wedderburn, one of the many tiny hamlets strung along the Oregon coast where lumber is the prime crop.

Their destination had been Wedderburn, where Gerry planned to visit a cousin who lived nearby. It was country Charlene knew well from the years before she had met Gerry. They stopped at the general store in Wedderburn and then looked for Gerry's cousin, but they were unable to find him. They turned back, toward Gold Beach, a state park located across the mouth of the Rogue River. As they approached the bridge, they saw a woman walking alone at the side of the road.

She walked erect, striding freely toward the bridge, her dark, hippie-style skirt swinging about her ankles with each step and clinging seductively to her thighs and buttocks as it hung from her swelling midriff. A cascade of long, dark hair fell almost to her hips.

There was no discussion with Charlene, no plan, no conspiracy. Gerry simply took his foot off the gas pedal, put it on the brake, and swung the van over to the side of the road, easing to a stop beside the long-striding young woman.

At the same time, Brad Wood was crossing the bridge in a car from the other direction. He had seen the woman walking away from the health food store in Wedderburn as he left town to take his wife to work at a resort in Gold Beach. Now on his return trip, Wood was planning to give the woman a lift.

The setting sun played tricks on Brad Wood. Later, he would report seeing a gold van with windows and horizontal striping on the sides pull off the road beside the pregnant woman. The van stopped only a moment or so, and when it rolled away, the woman was gone. Wood remembered she had been carrying a package.

Of course, what Brad Wood had actually seen was an aqua-white van with dark, unearthly mountains and an ugly black vulture roosting on one of the peaks painted on its side.

\*　　　\*　　　\*

"I want to give her a ride," Gerry announced.

Charlene looked at the woman. She was tiny and carried a shopping bag cradled in her arms. Black stockings covered her legs beneath the dark skirt. Her hips swung under the long garment. She wore a purple blouse. Charlene noticed the shoes. Hippie shoes. They resembled ballet slippers. The little hippie was obviously pregnant. Nothing would happen. She would be all right. She wasn't Gerry's type.

Gerry leaned across Charlene and shouted out the passenger window.

"Hey, want a ride?"

The little hippie smiled and got in.

"My old lady's pregnant, too," Gerry said proudly.

It was true, and there would be no abortion this time. Charlene had accepted terminating her pregnancy the last time only because they had not been married. Legally wed now, she thought, Charlene was determined to have this baby. There was no way she could know that Gerry had failed to legally divorce his last wife and that neither of her marriages to him was legal.

Charlene and the hippie woman talked over the din about the problems of pregnancy. Then, with his voice shielded by the loud music from the radio, Gerry announced his intentions.

"Baby, I want to take her." It was hard to hear in the van with the radio speakers adjusted the way Gerry liked them, blasting the country music. But Charlene got the message loud and clear.

*Baby, I want to take her.*

Did Gerry repeat himself or were the words merely echoing in her mind? In that dispassionate world where she watched these things take place, she was thinking, it's going to happen all over again.

This time, Charlene decided, it's different. This time the woman is pregnant, and she is back there sitting on the ice chest because she accepted a ride. There had been no trickery, no plans, no promises. One moment they were driving toward Gold Beach, and the next moment Gerry had stopped and was offering the woman a ride.

"No, Gerry, she's pregnant," Charlene said as loud as she dared.

But her protest forestalled nothing. Gerry had her change seats with him while the van was moving. She slid obediently into the driver's seat while Gerry crawled over the console into the rear with the pregnant woman.

Charlene moved into her two worlds then as she always did when these things happened. Gerry took his gun, the .357 Python, into the rear of the van with him. In the rear-view mirror, she saw him fumbling with the rope — the long yellow nylon rope he always carried in the back of the van.

The woman's hair was almost black and her skin was a smooth olive color. Not Gerry's usual type, Charlene thought again. Not thin and not blonde and not very young. Not his type at all. And she certainly never thought Gerry would have chosen a pregnant woman to be among the ranks of his doomed sex slaves.

Before long, the girl was on the bed and tied, lying on her stomach, face against the blankets. Charlene could see she was trying to shift her body to one side or the other, perhaps to take the strain off the baby in her womb.

The little hippie announced she needed to go to the bathroom. Gerry resumed his place behind the wheel of the van.

Across the river, toward Gold Beach, a broad meadow with a dirt road winding through it paralleled the highway. The field was covered with the dark green, heavy-bladed grass common to the country near the Oregon coast. Gerry drove the van into the center of the field. Charlene got out. She knew what was going to happen, and she didn't want to see it. She walked around the van, and from where she was standing, she spotted a lovely house in the distance. It had two stories with a long porch in front and several steps leading down to a sprawling front yard. The place was shuttered, and Charlene thought about how volatile the weather is along the Oregon coast in the winter.

She paced. The van was actually rocking, she noticed. Rocking and swaying. There was probably noise, but she didn't want to hear it. It was easier that way. No sobs, no screams, no pleading. She would hear none of it. After awhile, Gerry emerged, panting and perspiring.

"She couldn't do nothin' for me," he complained.

Charlene wondered what favors he'd demanded. Everything he asked of her? He was a master, magna cum lousy, of erotica. Certainly, he asked no less of his slaves than he did of his wife.

The woman's clothes were lying on the console between the front seats. Gerry told Charlene to hand them to him, piece by piece. In turn, he handed them to the naked woman and watched as she put each article back on. While the little hippie dressed, she complained again that she had to go to the bathroom.

"I'll take you to the bathroom," Gerry said.

Charlene knew what he meant.

But Gerry couldn't find the kind of place he was looking for. He drove back and forth over the Rogue River bridge, between Wedderburn and Gold Beach, parading repeatedly over the main streets of the coastal villages. Charlene reminded him he was making the van excessively visible with his constant trips back and forth through small towns. His one-van procession from Wedderburn to Gold Beach and back was bound to be noticed.

He drove the car off the road near the bank of the stream where it promptly became mired in the sands of the Rogue River. Gerry cursed and spluttered, perspiring as he shifted gears from low to reverse and back into low, violently jerking the van back and forth until it was free.

The afternoon was waning and it was getting dark. Charlene, huddled in the passenger's seat, recognized the country. She had visited the area on vacation trips with her family not once, but several times. When Gerry drove the van off the highway toward the beach, she knew there would be wooded hills on one side and a beach on the other.

Charlene thought about the little hippie, lying on the bed in the back of the van, her hands tied behind her and still complaining that she had to go to the bathroom.

She wondered how Gerry had managed with the girl in her pregnant state, with her bladder full. But then, he hadn't managed. And after trying, all he'd said was that she hadn't been able to do anything for him. Charlene could have told him that in the beginning. The little hippie just wasn't his type.

This is the place, Charlene thought, as the van turned off toward the beach. This is where it will happen all over again — where it will end for the pregnant hippie.

Charlene looked in back and saw the woman moving from side to side, shifting her weight. The woman's dark eyes were not angry but were clouded with fear and pain. Charlene knew she would not suffer much longer. It would soon be over.

She asked the little hippie if her hands were bound too tightly. The woman said no, she simply had to urinate.

Gerry finally stopped the van. He picked up the .357 magnum and put it in his pocket, then forced the girl out, telling her he was taking her to a place where she could go to the bathroom. The little hippie was whimpering as he led her away, past some rocky outcroppings on the beach and out of Charlene's sight.

Charlene got out of the van and waited in the deepening twilight. In the distance, she could hear cars and trucks driving along Highway 101.

The wait was short. Gerry never wasted any time when he brought these deadly trysts to their morbid conclusions. He was gone only about fifteen minutes. When he came back, he told her about hitting the little hippie with a rock and strangling her. "It was so easy," he said, sounding pleased. "I didn't know it could be so easy." He chuckled.

He said he wanted to bury the bag the woman had been carrying when they picked her up. Charlene handed it to him.

She had looked inside the bag while he was gone. It contained plastic toys, baby things. Watching Gerry walk back down the beach with the bag, the thought went through her mind. *Baby things.* He's going to bury the baby things.

But Gerry changed his mind at the last moment. Instead, they took the toys and things for the baby that would never be born and dropped them in a garbage can beside the highway.

\*     \*     \*

That night, pangs of remorse attacked Gerry. He ranted and raved. He said he was not good enough for Charlene — that he had spoiled everything. He wanted her to know he was sorry he had ruined their vacation.

Not once did he mention the life of the little hippie who had been striding freely on the highway between Wedderburn and Gold Beach. He was just sorry he had ruined the vacation.

Charlene was numb. She was beyond remorse. A permanent cloud of sadness and regret had already taken root in her in the sagebrush-covered hills of Nevada outside of Lovelock. The little girl with the long hair had sobbed for so long and Charlene had kept telling her, while stroking her beautiful hair, that everything would be all right. But Gerry had come and taken the girl away and killed her with a hammer and Charlene had lost something. She no longer cared much. It was easier to cope that way.

Lying back in the darkness, Charlene wondered how it would end. Someday it would be over, she knew. She also knew that Gerry would not stop before he was caught. He would kill and kill again. And she would probably keep doing her part, too. Why stop now? The girl with the long hair was already dead. The rest of them mattered little to her.

Suddenly, a frightening thought flashed through Charlene's mind and she shivered. *He doesn't need me anymore.* The little hippie had been all his. He had planned, engineered, and executed the rape and murder without any real help from her. Charlene wondered what Gerry might do if he realized he no longer needed her. Was she disposable like the rest of them? She could be dangerous to him, ruin him, help send him to jail or perhaps the gas chamber or a hangman's noose if she talked.

Charlene lived close enough to reality to know she would not be forgiven for her part in the murders. Not that she felt that she was really guilty. After all, she personally didn't kill anyone. She hadn't even witnessed any of the actual killings. She wasn't *that* kind of person.

She finally went to sleep, feeling safe for the time being, as safe as any woman married to a man like Gerry could feel. At least she was alive, which was more than could be said for seven other women who had briefly known Gerald Gallego.

# Ten

At four o'clock on the afternoon of June 9, 1980, a young commercial fisherman walked into the Curry County Sheriff's Department substation in Port Orford, Oregon, and reported that his "old lady" was missing. He told the deputy on duty that the woman was twenty-one years old and she'd been living with him for about three years. She was the mother of his two-year-old son, and she was several months pregnant.

The man was not overly worried. He explained, almost proudly, to the deputy that his girlfriend, Linda Aguilar, was independent and resourceful and capable of taking care of herself. Linda had been unhappy recently, he admitted, partly because their small child was getting on her nerves and partly because of her pregnancy, which was causing her discomfort. To him, she had seemed restless. If she did wander away, he said, she might simply disappear into the woods and live off the land for awhile. He knew she could do that, because for three years the two of them had hitchhiked together across the western United States, often without funds, and had never gone hungry. It's no big deal, he explained.

Although the report was not particularly alarming, the Curry County Sheriff's Department gave it more attention than a disappearance under similar circumstances would have received in a metropolitan area like Sacramento. Fewer people disappear in a small, rural town than in a big city.

Told by the young fisherman that Linda had possibly been hitchhiking in the Wedderburn area, deputies went there and questioned the owner of the health food store, who remembered the pregnant woman visiting his business late on the afternoon of June 7th.

A tavern owner in Gold Beach told the deputies that Linda Aguilar had been there with a friend sometime that afternoon and ordered a couple of beers. Some friends of hers reported seeing Linda during the afternoon and noticed nothing unusual. A consensus of Linda's friends held that she was often unhappy these days. She'd told numerous friends that she needed time to herself.

After three days of questioning people in Port Orford, Gold Beach, and Wedderburn, the deputies were convinced that Linda Aguilar had left home voluntarily. "It's apparent that Aguilar left her residence on her own and is not a missing person, as she was seen twice in the general area of her home," one of the deputies entered in his report on the incident.

Several friends claimed Linda and the young fisherman had been having an increasingly stormy relationship. Some said they had seen the young man slap her and punch her in public. Others told of Linda showing them bruises she'd said had been caused by his blows.

When more than a week passed and Linda had not been seen, the investigators did exactly what they should have done. They conducted more interviews, scores of them, in Wedderburn, Port Orford, and Gold Beach. One of the persons interviewed was Brad Wood, who gave the sheriff's department the following handwritten statement: "Taking my wife to work Saturday, June 7th, at approximately quarter to 6 p.m., I saw this girl walking north on the road, with a big smile on her face. I noticed her wearing a mid-length skirt and leotards (dark) and carrying some sort of package. I dropped my wife Leslie off at work. I was thinking of giving the girl a ride. Then I saw her getting picked up by a vehicle on the south end of the bridge. Best as I remember, the vehicle was a two-tone van, possibly gold and white." He signed the statement and it was added to an ever-growing pile of reports.

The killer's luck was holding.

*      *      *

Arel Kohnen and his wife, Carmen, middle-aged tourists from Germany, arrived at Gold Beach in their automobile at about seven o'clock on the evening of June 22, 1980. They opened the door of their car to let their dog run out and to take a walk on the beach whose scenery they so much admired.

Almost immediately, their dog trotted to a driftwood log high on the beach and lifted his leg. It had been a long drive, so his action provoked little attention. Soon, however, the Kohnens noticed that their dog was behaving strangely. Interrupting his expected activity, he started whimpering, then barking, all the while sniffing the area frantically with his nose close to the ground. The Kohnens hurried to their dog to see what was upsetting him.

The animal was now circling a blue piece of cloth which appeared to be part of a sweatshirt. When Arel Kohnen leaned over to pick it up, he was horrified by the sight of human flesh decomposing underneath.

The Kohnens recoiled and hurried back to their vehicle. Using their civilian band radio, they made contact with another "good buddy," an elderly couple traveling in a motor home. Within minutes the information reached the Curry County Sheriff's Department.

The corpse was listed as Jane Doe when it was taken to the Curry County Coroner's office for examination and autopsy. But everyone in Gold Beach, Port Orford, and Wedderburn knew it was Linda Aguilar. Long before an official announcement was made, the news swept through the isolated coastal communities.

The young woman's body had been found almost directly beneath a log which had served as her temporary tombstone during those twelve days she had been on the beach. She was lying on her back and her hands were bound behind her with a strand of nylon rope. The same type of rope had been used to bind her ankles. The rough suede purse and wallet found buried with the body contained all the identification the investigators needed. There were receipts, medical appointment notices, prescriptions, and memos all in the name of Linda Aguilar.

Despite the cool summer weather along the Oregon coast, the body was badly decomposed. It was taken to a morgue in the Curry County Sheriff's Department, and an autopsy was performed by a medical examiner. His first finding was that she had suffered two blows to the head, blows which had cracked her skull. Probing further, the medical examiner also discovered sand in Linda's mouth, throat, and lungs. That discovery made the cause of death horribly conclusive: She had been knocked out temporarily by blows to the head and buried beneath the sand of Gold Beach while still alive. With her hands and feet bound, she had no chance of digging herself out. Desperately gasping for air, Linda must have inhaled sand as she battled for her life to the last breath during those final agonizing moments underground.

*     *     *

Even prior to the discovery of her body, as the days passed without news about Linda Aguilar, anxiety had already mounted in the small and close-knit coastal communities of Southern Oregon. The young fisherman who had reported her disappearance began to notice growing hostility toward him, as friends and neighbors would go out of their way to avoid him. Stories about his abuse of Linda grew and were no doubt exaggerated as they passed from mouth to mouth. Disgusted and dejected, the fisherman, taking the couple's young son with him, left the community a few days before Linda's body was found.

He made no attempt to hide, and deputies from the Curry County Sheriff's Department quickly located him in Redding, California. When they talked to him, the fisherman soon realized that he had become a prime murder suspect. He returned to Wedderburn with the deputies, promising to help in any way he could. A rapidly accumulating file of circumstantial evidence was pointing to him as the murderer of Linda.

From the broken crockery found in the trailer shared by the fisherman and Linda to the man who told an Oregon State Police investigator he'd seen the young fellow "beat the shit out of Linda's dog," the chain of circumstantial evidence against the young man continued to expand daily and link him closer to the crime.

Another resident of the trailer park in Port Orford where the fisherman and Linda lived told investigators Linda had been chased into her trailer by her boyfriend shortly after midnight on May 2nd. He had been seething with anger, and Linda was so terrified she hid in her neighbor's bathroom to get away from him.

The neighbor said Linda had lived with her for two weeks, and that in spite of their rift, she continued to see the fisherman. As the interrogation progressed, the neighbor confessed that she and her husband had joined their house guest and her boyfriend in group sex during Linda's two-week stay. She went on to say that the fisherman was obsessed with sex. He had once followed her into the shower, suggesting a game of hide and seek in the nude.

Most damaging was the neighbor's claim of what the fisherman said when asked if he thought his girlfriend would return. "No, she won't," he reportedly told the woman. "It's too late." The neighbor also said she noticed that the boyfriend's knuckles were bruised. When she asked him how they had been hurt, he told her he'd bruised them on his fishing boat.

One of the fisherman's few remaining friends on the Oregon coast told police the young man had been depressed because he had "caught Linda sleeping with somebody else."

The report was another nail in the scaffold of rumors which was rising in Port Orford and its neighboring communities. A noose of circumstantial evidence was tightening around the neck of the not-so-innocent-yet-not-guilty fisherman.

The case against him was made even stronger on the night of July 1st. Two deputies went to the trailer shared by the fisherman and Linda Aguilar. They had a search warrant that would enable them to spray luminal, a substance which acquires a fluorescent glow in the dark when it contacts blood stains which have been washed or wiped away and are otherwise not visible.

At 10:30 p.m., the officers started spraying in the north bedroom of the trailer and almost immediately noticed a fluorescent stain under the window. There was more blood outside the bedroom door and on a chair in the living room, and blood speckling was present on some walls. The officers took the chair and small hatchet found in back of the trailer as evidence.

The fisherman, who admitted to "grabbing and pushing" Linda once in a while, agreed to take a polygraph test. The officers then took him to the Shasta County Sheriff's Department in Redding to be tested.

During the examination, the fisherman was asked four critical questions. "Were you personally involved in causing Linda Aguilar's death?" "Did you strike one or more of the blows that caused Linda Aguilar's death?" "Were you present when the blows were struck that caused Linda Aguilar's death?" "Do you know who struck the blows that caused Linda Aguilar's death?" His answer to each question was "no." It was determined by the polygraph expert that the fisherman was not being truthful in his answers to any of the four questions. A second polygraph was made later in the day. That time, the results were termed "inconclusive."

\*      \*      \*

Far back in the police files was another report, long since filed away. It told about an interview with Brad Wood of Gold Beach. Questioned at police headquarters, Wood positively identified a picture of Linda Aguilar as the woman who was picked up by the van. Unable to provide additional information on his own, Wood agreed to be hypnotized. Authorities were hoping to be given more details of what he'd seen from the Rogue River bridge late on the afternoon of June 7th.

Under hypnosis, Wood noted that the young woman had no luggage and looked as if she had not intended to go far. Concerning the van that picked her up, he remembered that it had tinted or perhaps one-way windows in the rear and on both sides. He recalled a man driving who was wearing a white T-shirt. And as the van passed, the driver had looked over his shoulder, as though talking to someone in the rear. The man had a dark complexion with no beard, and he had both hands on the steering wheel. A smaller person was sitting beside him. Wood didn't know if the passenger was a man or woman. The passenger had also turned and talked to someone in the rear. Although it was light outside at the time, it had been dark in the van and Wood hadn't been able to see the people too clearly. He remembered the van being exceptionally clean. He could not remember seeing any numbers or letters on the license plate.

A search for a gold and white van was launched. But for the most part, the investigators concentrated their interest on the young fisherman. An Oregon state trooper noted that the fisherman showed a "remarkable lack of interest" in the apprehension of the victim's murderer and that he had made little or no effort to search for her prior to the discovery of her body. He had, in fact, left the state of Oregon prior to its discovery and had, on numerous occasions, expressed the wish to get on with his new life in California.

On July 16th, in a neighboring state, an aqua-white van with unworldly paintings on its sides pulled up in front of a bar in West Sacramento. The driver, a short-haired man with a stocky build, and his companion, a petite woman, went inside and stayed until closing time.

95

The next day, the bartender, an attractive blonde who looked younger than her thirty-four years, was reported missing.

# Eleven

Charlene and Gerald Gallego had returned to California long before the blonde bartender was reported missing. Charlene continued to live in her own world, halfway between dream and reality. Gerry began smoking pot regularly, and when he did, she joined him. Actually, she preferred cocaine. She would later justify its use with the rationalization that it was needed to make life with Gerry more tolerable.

Still employed by the food distributor, Charlene's relationship with her immediate superior was rapidly deteriorating. She was the only woman in sales, and she believed her boss was sorry he had hired her. Charlene felt that she was expected to keep her place — a "woman's place" — in which she should listen during sales meetings but not talk. Her ever-increasing dependence on drugs also contributed to her deteriorating position with the firm.

After Gerry's outburst of remorse "for ruining their vacation," there was never again any mention of the Gold Beach murder. The ghost of Linda Aguilar was another member of a growing club which stayed in the shadowy recesses of Charlene's increasingly troubled mind. As for Gallego, he was more unpredictable than ever, his moods swinging from euphoric highs to agonizing lows in seconds. Often he was gone all night, returning home reeking of booze and dope just as Charlene was leaving for work. His recreation was Charlene's recreation:

beer or booze or grass, softball games, fishing expeditions. Rape and murder.

Booze was not Charlene's preferred high. But when she drank, she drank to get drunk. Whatever refuge she found in an alcoholic haze wasn't as pleasant as the coke, though. After every drunk came the inevitable depression.

She and Gerry often went fishing in the evening along the banks of the Sacramento River, finding remote areas his customers at the bar had told him about. Usually, the fishing trips were nightmares. Charlene had known nothing about fishing before meeting Gerry, but it was she who would catch the fish whenever they went. With each catch of hers, his mood would darken. She didn't do anything right, he would hiss. She just had stupid luck. On these trips they would drink a great deal. Usually it was straight vodka out of plastic cups they kept in the van.

The night of July 16th was a particularly bad one. Neither Gerry nor Charlene had any luck catching any keepers. What fish did bite were small, striped bass not worth the trouble. In the early evening hours, Gallego drank more and more, and Charlene matched him drink for drink. In her pregnant condition the booze nauseated her, and as she returned to the van she vomited violently. Woozy and exhausted, she leaned against the van and waited for an outraged Gerry to lash out at her. He never liked it when she got sick.

But his reaction was unexpected. He kept quiet and drove silently a short distance, then stopped the van and got out, pacing back and forth in the gathering darkness. She followed him. He was crying convulsively. "Baby, I'm no good for you," he sobbed. "You just don't know what I'm doing to you. I'm just not good enough for you. You should find someone better."

He continued a raving confession while he sobbed, admitting to the relationship with Evelyn Smith, detailing his infidelity while Charlene held him in her arms.

"It's all right, honey," she said. "I understand."

She didn't understand. But she held and consoled him. If there'd been an occasional suspicion, she had no real knowledge of Gerry's involvement with another woman — at least, not with a woman who was still living. She didn't want to hear the details, didn't want to know more, but he kept talking, and she told him softly that she didn't care. As they walked arm in arm, she asked him if he was in love with the other woman. Still sobbing, he said he was not but that the woman was so much in love with him that she'd attempted suicide when she learned he was married.

The confession continued as they walked back and forth over the dusty surface of the rich loam of the delta. Seeing him so weak brought out her maternal instincts, the same instincts that make so many women fall for cruel, weak, self-pitying men. "I love you, Gerry," she purred.

When the evening sun dropped over the shoulder of the distant coastal hills, a chill came over the valley and they drove away, passing the river town of Freeport as they traveled over the back roads and away from the twisting bank of the river. Gerry calmed down by degrees until, as they entered West Sacramento, they passed an inviting tavern and he suggested they stop for a drink.

They walked inside and ordered a Black Russian for her and a shot of tequila for him. Before long, Gerry was talking shop with the bartender. Gerry hardly seemed to notice the second bartender at all. She chatted with Charlene between serving rounds of drinks, moving back and forth as her work demanded and stopping now and then for a few words.

She was a slender woman, blonde and pretty, reminding Charlene a little of herself.

Gerry became involved with the male bartender and a group of men who had been frog gigging along the river bank. Charlene played a game of pool with Gerry and introduced him to her new-found friend behind the bar.

The evening began to blur a little for Charlene. The male bartender played pool with Gerry and eventually left the tavern, explaining that he had been off duty for some time but had stayed around to help Virginia, the woman bartender, with the early evening rush. Charlene's conversation with the lady bartender continued sporadically.

As the evening wore on, just about everybody shot pool with Gerry, but soon, he and Charlene were the only customers left in the tavern. Virginia was cleaning up — washing and polishing glasses, putting away bottles, taking care of all the little chores required at the end of a shift.

It was two o'clock, closing time, and Charlene went to the bathroom before they left. When she returned, Gerry was muttering softly so the lady bartender couldn't hear, "You know, we could take this joint off and her, too." "Gerry, come on," Charlene whispered. "Don't be crazy. Look, there are people out in the parking lot." She talked about David, Gerry's brother, who was still doing time for armed robbery, and she recalled the stories Gerry had told her about committing robberies and how he and David had been careful at first and then began robbing places on the spur of the moment. He had explained it was their carelessness which led to their arrest, conviction, and imprisonment.

"Man, you're getting reckless," she said, shaking her head in bewilderment.

She got him outside and then remembered she'd left her coat inside.

"Well, go get it," he said in a cranky tone.

She went to the door of the tavern, which was locked by then, and knocked. "Virginia, it's Charlene. I left my coat inside."

Virginia asked where she'd left it. Then the bartender came to the door, unlocked it, and handed the coat to Charlene.

"Thanks, Virginia," she said. "It was nice meeting you. Maybe we'll see you again."

She went back to the van, where Gerry was still muttering about how he could take the place and the bartender, too. He was out of his mind, Charlene thought, drunk and crazed. Even with all the drinks she'd put down, she knew this was crazy because there were still people in the parking lot. And then, all of a sudden, the other people were gone and the van was alone in the lot. Gerry began driving and Charlene thought it was over. They were going home and everything would be fine.

Then, Virginia stepped out of the bar, locking the door behind her. She walked toward her car with Gerry staring at her and Charlene saying, "Gerry, she's leaving. Come on, now. Let's go home."

But Gerry had other things on his mind. He stopped the van next to the bartender's car. The .357 Python was in his hand and suddenly he was outside, standing at Virginia's partly opened window. She was sitting behind the steering wheel, looking at Gerry with dark comprehension. When Gerry opened the car door, the woman stepped out.

Gerry, with the gun in his hand, was standing beside the woman under the parking lot light, clearly visible. They talked, and then he opened the back of the van and she climbed inside.

Charlene jumped out of the van. She hurried over to the woman's car and with a rag wiped clean the door handle so there would be no fingerprints.

When she returned to the van, she heard Gerry saying to Virginia that she could get into the bar if she wanted to. But Virginia told him there was a key that only worked one way and that once she locked up only another person with the other key could open the door.

Virginia switched topics and soon started talking about her children. She begged Gerry to let her call her baby sitter.

The bartender was sitting in back and Charlene was in the passenger seat while Gerry drove. A small car entered the parking lot as the van pulled slowly away. Charlene heard herself asking Virginia if it was someone she knew. Virginia said she didn't think so.

They drove up onto I-80 and headed east.

"Where are we going?" Charlene asked.

"Back to Woodhollow," he answered.

Woodhollow. Their home.

"No, Gerry, you're not taking her to our house. That's stupid."

"I'll keep her in the van," he explained. "You can go inside."

Soon, Charlene was driving and Gerry was in the back, tying the woman's hands and feet. After the task was completed, Gerry changed seats with Charlene again. The gun was on the floor in front of them. Gerry was telling the woman to shut up, but she only kept quiet for a short time before starting up again, chattering nervously about her children, always about her children.

Gerry told her to shut up or he would kill her.

"Why don't you just go ahead and kill me now?" She taunted. At the house, Gerry parked in the driveway.

Charlene went inside. She was disgusted. Was she supposed to sit in their house and wait? She sat by the window in a rocking chair. She could hear them — not what was being said, but the muffled sounds of a man and woman having an argument. She opened the back door and called out.

"Gerry, I can hear you two all the way in the house."

She turned on the television, picked up her cat, and sat down again. She watched an old movie, trying unsuccessfully to keep her mind on the plot.

Charlene was confused at the prospect of Gerry bringing his fantasy home. Obviously, nothing they had together meant anything to him anymore. It was all gone. Long ago, he had told her he needed her. But out there, in the van, was more evidence that he didn't. The thoughts reeled through her mind, pushing away her awareness of the cat in her lap, the old movie, the woman in the van, the sounds of her struggling, the knowledge of what would soon take place.

The back door opened softly and Gerry walked in. Charlene was drawn out of her thoughts by his voice. "Come on, let's go."

The television set was still on when they left. Charlene sat in the passenger seat and Virginia was in the back. It was dark in the front of the van, but it was light in the back. The woman was whimpering, repeating the same phrases over and over.

"Just kill me. Why don't you just go ahead and kill me?"

Virginia had been brutally violated and she didn't want to live any longer. She was lying on her back on the bed where seven young women had rested before they died, and Charlene saw her in a strange sort of light that didn't seem real.

"I could hear you," Charlene whined. "All the way inside."

Gerry explained they had to take Virginia all the way back to West Sacramento near the tavern where she worked.

The woman in the back was still talking about her kids. Then, her voice changed tone and she was begging again to be killed.

"Gerry, God," Charlene finally groaned. "I just can't take it." Gerry barked at Virginia to shut up. Then he told Charlene that he was taking the woman to a place where they had fished in the past. He was still driving, and he turned off the freeway to a rural road Charlene would not forget. "Get in the driver's seat," Gerry said.

They traded places. He told Charlene he was going back to kill the woman, so she should turn up the radio to drown out the noise.

"Don't turn around," he said as he climbed into the back. "I'll close the curtain."

She sat alone in the front in the darkness with the radio blasting and Virginia's voice still playing a broken record in her memory: *Just kill me. Why don't you just kill me now?* That's what Gerry was going to do. He was back there killing her just as she had asked him to do.

There was no gunshot. Gerry had learned on Gold Beach just a month and ten days earlier how easy it was to strangle a woman. He didn't need a gun or a hammer, only his hands, the same evil hands which he had used to violate so many women, including his own daughter.

Charlene drove on, through the darkness.

Finally, Gerry climbed back up front. A few minutes later, he pushed the curtain aside and peeked back at the prone and now silent figure on the bed. He asked Charlene if she could turn the van around on the narrow, rocky road. When she said she wasn't sure, he changed places with her. ,

Charlene felt drained. She was thinking that the woman in back was finally dead. At least she was quiet. "God, Gerry," she gasped, "is she dead?"

"Yeah. She's dead."

Charlene thought about the gun, the .357 Python he kept in a holster. He had fired it earlier at the river when they were fishing. He liked to shoot guns. It made him feel macho.

"You're not going to shoot her?" she asked, apprehensively.

"Naw. It was easy, like the other one. Now all we've got to do is find a place to get rid of her," he said in the way one would discuss dumping the garbage.

As the curtains flapped when the van rolled over a deep rut, Charlene reluctantly caught a glimpse of Gerry's handy work. The woman was on the bed, lying still, so very still. Her face was drained of all color. Her neck was swollen like a watermelon and purplish red. There was a great blackened bruise on her neck below her chin where Gerry had broken her hyoid bone, the inevitable by-product of the violence of strangulation. They stopped on a levee road they both knew. Dawn was cracking the tops of the Sierra Nevada in the east and the sky was no longer jet black.

Gerry stopped the van and hopped out. As he opened the back door of the van the curtain flapped open wide. Once again, Charlene caught a glimpse of Virginia, this time of her bare leg. She quickly turned back around and looked straight ahead as Gerry started pulling the body toward him. She could hear the sound of the body being dragged, scraping against the floor of the van. Then she heard a thump, an awful thump.

Then there was silence. She waited.

When she saw Gerry coming up out of the riverbed a few minutes later, she automatically switched seats.

They rode back to Woodhollow. A cleaning job awaited Charlene, and Gerry went around collecting all the incriminating evidence.

Later that morning, he was impatient that it was taking her so long to clean up. He had remembered it was a special day for him.

"You're not going to fuck this up," he warned. "You're not going to fuck up my birthday."

They had a private party at Zorba's, a Greek restaurant in Sacramento, on the frontage road of Highway 80. Afterward, Gerry wanted to return to the river, explaining to Charlene that when the police start working on the case they could discover that the fishing line he'd used to tie up the bartender had come from their reels.

"Leave her alone, Gerry," Charlene pleaded. "Just leave her alone."

Back home, Gerry changed the line on the reels and started getting rid of Virginia's clothes and jewelry that had been left in the van. Charlene thought some more about the woman being a lot like her. Some of Virginia's jewelry even looked like hers. And the bartender had been wearing slacks which were like a pair Charlene owned. The comparisons frightened Charlene. The recurring thought that Gerry was perfectly capable of killing her, too, haunted her that night.

*　　*　　*

When Charlene returned home from work one day a week later, Gerry greeted her with a strange smile.

"The police called here today," he said calmly. "They left a message for you."

Charlene was startled. Gerry had warned her that the police might get mixed up in the Yolo County episode with the lady bartender. Still, the prospect of being questioned by police shocked her. The cops had never been near them before, not ever.

"What do they want?" she asked uneasily.

"They just want to talk to you. A detective named Trujillo or something like that. Just don't tell him anything."

# Twelve

*Lt. Biondi — Homicide*

At four o'clock in the morning on July 17th, Bill Cannon, a regular customer at the Sail Inn, drove past the bar and noticed that Virginia Mochel's car was still in the lot. He didn't see any lights in the place but stopped and knocked on the door anyway.

No one answered. He nosed around Virginia's car. The window was down partway on the driver's side. Maybe Virginia had gone off to breakfast with some friends. She did that now and then. Cannon looked around a little more, then went home.

He knew Virginia would not have left with a man. That wasn't her style. She was an attractive woman, and more than one of her men customers speculated now and then on her ability in bed. But Virginia didn't encourage any of them. She understood she couldn't work behind the bar if word got out she was an easy mark.

At thirty-four, Virginia Mochel had carved a small place for herself in this lower-middle-class river community across from the state capital. Petite, pretty, and personable, she was genuinely interested in her customers and easy to talk to. A good bartender, she never got the recipe for a French 75 mixed up with that of a Tom Collins. With a sympathetic ear and a sure hand with drinks, she had developed a loyal following at the Sail Inn.

Thousands of people are reported missing in this country every day, and each missing-persons case demands a different treatment and degree of urgency. A husband known for alcoholic Saturday nights may develop a familiar pattern of behavior. Police will search the records of the local hospitals, accident reports, and drunk arrests, and most of the time, they will produce the missing man within hours. A disgruntled wife reported missing by her husband may well have left behind a note, which he has not revealed, telling him she has finally found a man who doesn't snore. Since runaway spouses are not breaking any laws, searching for them and finding them is more often than not a waste of the department's time. On the other hand, missing toddlers require and get immediate attention and an all-out effort by every available officer. So did a missing mother who clearly had no plans of deserting her children.

The baby sitter for Virginia Mochel's two children showed remarkable restraint when she waited until three o'clock on the afternoon of July 18th to call police. When she finally called the authorities, the baby sitter told a deputy that Virginia had not come home from work that morning and that her children had not heard from her. The baby sitter said that such behavior was out of character for the attentive and conscientious mother.

A patrol car was dispatched to the Sail Inn, and a deputy spoke with the day manager, who told him Virginia had come to work at six o'clock the previous evening in good spirits. Her car was still parked in the tavern's parking lot.

Virginia's twelve-year-old daughter told officers she was worried about her mother. Before going to work the previous afternoon, her mother had been happy and healthy and she'd not said anything about plans to be home late.

Patrol officers made all the right moves. They procured a photograph of the missing woman and checked all local hospitals. They also searched local morgues for any new "Jane Does" that might fit Virginia Mochel's description. When they came up empty-handed, they broadcast an "all points" bulletin for the missing woman.

Yolo County Sheriff's Deputies Dave Trujillo and Rick Mayoral were assigned to investigate the case. Instinct, the raw hunch which is always a part of police work, told them their investigation would probably end on a downbeat. They sensed tragedy, like all good cops do. Experience whispered in morbid tones, telling them the lady bartender at the Sail Inn would not be found alive.

Trujillo and Mayoral found Bill Cannon, who worked for the Sacramento Convention Center and got off work around midnight. He usually stopped by the Sail Inn on the way home and often didn't get out of the place before the two o'clock closing hour.

Cannon considered Virginia a friend, confidante, and sister confessor. Often at night, after visiting with her at the bar, Cannon waited until closing to escort her to her car in the parking lot. A woman couldn't be too careful in West Sacramento, which was getting crowded with seedy motels and hotels.

Cannon told Trujillo that on the night in question he noticed a couple at the bar who seemed to know some of the regular customers. Both the man and woman shot some pool, although the man spent more time at the pool table than the woman, who mainly just sat and chatted with Virginia across the bar. He hadn't liked the man, Cannon said. As the evening wore on, the man became pretty drunk and a little offensive. He had patted Virginia on the bottom a couple of times when she was near the pool table. "She kinda pushed him away, telling him not to do that," Cannon said.

No one at the Sail Inn treated Virginia that way. Later, the man had tried to buy Virginia a drink, and he became quarrelsome when she refused. He acted insulted that she wouldn't drink with him. "He told Virginia a bartender should sample the wares with the customers," Cannon continued. "Virginia said she didn't have to do that. You see, she'd given up drinking."

Cannon said he shot a game of pool with the troublemaker. "I'm no pool player and he was pretty good. He kept talking about being from Texas."

Also at the bar that night were half a dozen fellows who had been frogging. Trujillo tracked them down and found out that they'd been there early and then returned right after Virginia closed. When they knocked on the door, she had told them firmly the bar was closed. Then she opened the door just a crack to examine and admire their frogs. Virginia was like that, they told the investigator. She was nice, but no fool.

Like most neighborhood bars, the Sail Inn didn't entertain many strangers. When Trujillo and Mayoral began tracking down the folks who were there on the night of the 16th and the wee hours of the 17th, they didn't have much trouble locating most of them. The froggers were regulars at the bar. But one customer that night, a Yolo County fireman, didn't get there much. He had arrived with a couple of other firemen who visited the bar often. One frogger hadn't liked the fireman at all. He regarded him as raunchy and foul-mouthed. "If I was suspicious of anyone, it would be him," the regular told the investigators.

Most of the customers remembered a white-haired man, maybe sixty-five years old, whom they had not seen before. He was a little paunchy and a bit argumentative. He seemed to have an opposite opinion on most everything discussed that night. No one liked the older man. They remembered he gave Virginia a close inspection and seemed to like what he saw.

Trujillo located the older man. He told the detective he'd been in the Sail Inn once or twice before. He didn't live in the area but visited Sacramento on business. A few days after July 17th, he said he'd returned to the tavern and noticed a sign behind the bar announcing that donations were being accepted for Virginia Mochel's family. That was the first he knew about the bartender's disappearance.

Trujillo also talked with the man who had been tending bar with Virginia earlier in the evening. He, too, recalled the couple who played pool. The guy worked in a North Sacramento bar and his name was Feil.

The investigator found Stephen Feil's telephone number and called the house. Feil himself answered. He remembered being in the Sail Inn but not very much else, confessing he'd had too much to drink. His wife, Charlene, would know more about the evening. Trujillo left a message for her to call.

Charlene returned Trujillo's call on the evening of July 23rd and the conversation was brief. She said she and her husband, Stephen, had been at the Sail Inn Bar the night of July 16th after fishing. She said they had both been drinking and she couldn't remember too much of what had happened.

As Trujillo and his partner, Rick Mayoral, traced through Virginia Mochel's past, they discovered she had been married and that the parting with her husband had been stormy. He had, just before the breakup, visited the bar where she was working and thrown a bar stool through a window. Rick Mayoral found the husband and talked to him. The man said he had no bad feelings about Virginia, and he appeared to be genuinely concerned about her.

The investigators were getting a lot of help. Daily, the Sail Inn regulars gathered on the banks of one or another of the many sloughs and channels in the Sacramento River Delta and searched for Virginia's body. They were convinced she was dead, and they thought she deserved a proper burial.

The summer passed, and nothing was heard or seen of Virginia Mochel. One of her children, the twelve-year-old girl, went to live with her father. The younger child went to live with another relative. Regulars at the Sail Inn, faithful to their pretty bartender, continued to scour the riversides, searching for her body. Then, as the summer waned, they gave up.

\*    \*    \*

On October 2, 1980, a fisherman walking along the riverbank near Freeport saw something unusual in the water. A brief inspection of his find sent him to the nearest phone where he called the Yolo County Sheriff's Department.

Dave Trujillo examined the body, or what was left of it by then, nearly three months after Virginia Mochel had disappeared. The pretty bartender from the Sail Inn had been left nude, wearing only a couple of rings. Her arms were bound behind her with fishing line.

Trujillo, who was normally easygoing, had become intense and determined while working on the Virginia Mochel case. When her body was found, he stayed up one night reviewing the entire case file from the beginning.

It was then that Trujillo noticed something. *Fishing line.* He remembered a group of guys who had been at the Sail Inn that night had been frogging. But froggers didn't use fishing line. Going through his reports he remembered the couple who had been fishing. *Feil.* Stephen and Charlene Feil had been fishing early in the evening on the 16th before they visited the Sail Inn. He decided to talk to them again.

Trujillo called Charlene, discovered she had moved, located her new phone number, and asked her to drop in to the Yolo County Sheriff's substation on Third Street in Broderick, just across the river from Sacramento.

Charlene Feil came at once but did not provide much new information. She appeared to be cooperative and articulate, answering all the questions as best she could. She remembered the froggers. They were loud and noisy. She remembered playing pool. But she had trouble remembering details. She admitted to having drunk too much. "I was pretty far gone," she confessed.

To the detective, she seemed candid.

"How did you get home?" Trujillo asked.

"I drove."

"How did you make it if you were that far gone?"

"By the grace of God," she said coolly.

# The Father

*I saw my chance at the jail and hit the guard. It took him by surprise, but he came back after me swinging. I beat him up pretty bad. He tried to grab his gun but I always made sure he never drew it for I kept hitting him in the face, kicking him in the groin and I bounced his head off the bars. I pushed his head through the window. I hit him so hard that I drove his head into the plaster. He didn't have a chance after that and I kept reminding myself I was going to kill the next cop that ever tried arresting me. I finally got his gun away from him, and I told him I would kill him if he didn't drive me out of town. He was afraid and he kept begging me not to kill him. I made him drive me through a couple of towns and him still begging for his life. I told him I wouldn't, but I knew I was and I could hardly wait to kill him.*

From the death row statement of Gerald Albert Gallego
Mississippi State Prison
Jackson, Mississippi, 1954

# Thirteen

Midnight had come and gone. The Founder's Day Dance was over and the orchestra had gone home. Andy Beal and his date left the Carousel Restaurant and crossed through the dark parking lot. It was then that Andy spotted Craig Miller and Mary Beth Sowers sitting in the back seat of a big Oldsmobile.

Craig and Mary Beth would have been hard to miss because a bright dome light was shining above them. Andy wondered what they were doing in a car like that. They were all just college kids who drove old wrecks — aging Honda Civics or VW bugs or ancient Chevys — sometimes held together with baling wire. The silver-blue Olds Cutlass was classy transportation.

A few minutes earlier, Craig had suggested that they all go to Andy's place and continue the party. Andy had turned thumbs down on the idea, knowing that his neighbors would not appreciate the sounds of a college party in the wee hours of the morning.

Andy now decided to play a joke — just a little prank which would give them all a laugh. He quickened his pace, moving ahead of his date, and climbed in on the driver's side of the Olds and sat down behind the wheel.

Not until he was all the way in the car did Andy see the older man sitting in the passenger's seat. The man did not seem threatening or angry or even surprised. Andy glanced back at Craig. His friend's face was tight, drawn, and serious.

"You don't belong in this car, Andy," Craig said firmly, his voice steady and calm.

The joke suddenly didn't seem so funny to Andy. He climbed out of the car. Before he had a chance to move away, he was challenged by a short blonde.

"What the fuck are you doing in my car?" she shouted.

Stunned by the words and the savage way they were delivered, an embarrassed Andy tried to apologize. "I didn't mean . . ." he stammered, " . . . anything . . . I'm sorry."

The harsh words coming from the woman didn't fit her looks. She was barely five feet tall and slender to the point of being skinny, weighing maybe ninety pounds. When her roundhouse right, a stinging slap, landed on the cheek of the six-foot-four, 225-pound Andy Beal, she was standing on her tiptoes.

Andy's youthful face flushed.

Andy did not know that moments before, Craig Miller and Mary Beth Sowers had been confronted by the man sitting in the front seat of the Olds. Neither did he know that the stubby man had pointed a gun at Craig and Mary Beth and forced them into the back seat of the two-door car. Not until their captor and the blonde were situated in the front seat had Craig made his desperate gesture. He had thrown the keys to Mary Beth's Honda out the passenger's window. The blonde had turned on him savagely. "That was a stupid thing to do," she hissed. She had left the car and gone around the other side looking for the keys when Andy Beal jumped behind the wheel.

Andy also could not know that Craig was trying to save his life. Craig undoubtedly wanted Andy out of the car and away from the muzzle of the gun the passenger held in his hand. In the confusion of Andy being behind the wheel, it might have been possible for Craig to grab the man from behind and, with Andy's help, subdue him. But there was the gun to consider.

If it went off, it could kill his friend, and maybe his beloved Mary Beth in the process.

Andy didn't like getting hit, even by a pint-sized woman. "Bitch," he muttered as he backed away.

"Whatever," the blonde said arrogantly, pushing past Andy to her rightful place behind the wheel.

Andy walked to where his girlfriend was watching. He turned around in time to see the blonde driving the Olds out of the lot.

"There's something awfully wrong here," Andy told his date.

His gaze instinctively dropped to the license plate.

\*     \*     \*

Charlene was worried. Experience had taught her what would happen next. She moved automatically and dutifully, the way she had in all the other nightmares. These people they had just kidnapped were not like the others, though. Not like the children from the shopping centers. Not like the little hippie. Not even like the lady bartender.

The young man in the back of the car was someone Charlene might have dated had she not thrown her past away. He was handsome, polite, and well bred. And she could have been that girl, that pretty and poised girl, Charlene thought. These were good kids. College kids. Kids with bright futures. The kind of kids her parents would have wanted her to be like.

Beside her, Gerry was pointing the little gun at the pretty girl in the silk dress and the good-looking young man in the blue suit. Gerry didn't seem fazed by what had just happened in the parking lot.

Charlene was still worried, however. "I'm sure the big guy in the parking lot saw our license number," she said. "And I can't believe he didn't see the gun."

Maybe she could talk Gerry out of it. Maybe, just maybe, if they stopped the car a block or two away from the shopping center and told the two kids to get out, that it was all a joke, the incident would be written off as a prank and everyone concerned would be safe. The kids and she and Gerry would go on with their lives. Gerry had to realize how dangerous it would be to proceed with his plan now. He *had* to know.

"Shut up and drive," he said sternly.

She drove, but she didn't stop talking. "That guy was *looking*, Gerry. He must have seen the license plate."

"Just drive."

"Where to?"

"Back out to the freeway."

She found an on ramp and turned east on U.S. 50 where the highway begins to rise and wind through gentle hills on its way to the Sierra Nevada.

Gerry was drunk, and he was mean. He could always be mean, of course. But with hard liquor coursing through his veins, he was savage and unthinking. He asked the young man in the back seat how much money he had on him. Craig Miller answered. It wasn't very much. Under twenty dollars.

Gerry told the boy to hand over his wallet. Then he turned to the girl. "Why are you going with a bum like this?" he asked evenly.

The girl said something Charlene didn't catch. Charlene was distracted. She was still thinking about the big kid she'd slapped. "He must have seen the plate," she said again.

Gerry ignored her.

The road swung south, a long, sweeping curve rising sharply, then turned east again as the slope gentled. A highway sign indicated they were approaching Bass Lake Road.

"Turn off here," Gerry said.

Charlene followed the off ramp to a road which dead-ended at a farmhouse. A snarling Gerry ordered her to turn around. She drove back under the freeway to a graveled road which twisted through the foothills.

"Slow," Gerry warned. "Go slow."

That was the tipoff. Gerry always became acutely conscious of the traffic laws when something bad was going to happen. The nightmare was about to begin all over again.

Charlene drove until Gerry told her to turn off the lights and park on the shoulder of the road. All the while, Gerry kept the gun pointed at the couple in the back seat. The girl had been quiet, but once or twice, Craig Miller had asked Gerry to take him and let the girl go. Charlene knew her husband had altogether different plans.

Charlene heard something about the boy's shoes. She didn't understand why, but Gerry told him to take them off. So he couldn't run away? Then, ordering the boy out of the car, Gerry followed behind him.

Craig Miller walked to the roadside in front of the car. Then, while he continued to move slowly away, Gerry shot him in the back of the head.

Charlene was outraged! Gerry shot him right in front of her! Right in the path illuminated by the headlights. That had never happened before. Not ever!

The handsome college kid could have never felt the shot, could have never known what happened. He dropped face down to the dry, brown grass next to the road. Gerry stood over the kid and pointed the gun at his head, then fired two more shots. Leaving the still-warm corpse on the side of the road, he climbed into the back seat of the car next to the stunned girl in the silk dress and told Charlene to get going.

"Where to?" Charlene asked flatly.

"To my place," he answered.

Charlene and Gerry had been separated for several months. He had moved to a succession of motels and then to a seedy apartment in an older section of Sacramento. Charlene had gone back to her parents' home in the prestigious neighborhood where they lived. The van had been sold.

Out of the blue, Gerry had called Charlene that day, suggesting that they get together. She had agreed, and now, they were doing it again.

As Charlene drove to Gerry's apartment, a part of her was empathizing with the fear, the terror, the paralyzing fright that had overwhelmed Mary Beth Sowers. Another part of her was hating the girl in the shimmering party dress.

At that moment, Gerry had his arms around the girl, cooing in her ear. "Do you want to be my Sally Jo tonight?" he asked softly. "How would you like that?"

Gerry would take her in more ways than the girl knew was possible before the night was over, Charlene knew. He would take her just as surely as the sun would rise in the morning. Nothing could stop him. And when he was through with this lovely girl, she would die.

*       *       *

Andy Beal's first impulse when he saw the Olds pull out of the parking lot had been to jump into his own car and give chase. He sensed that Craig and Mary Beth were in that automobile against their will. The time to do something about it was immediately.

But Andy hesitated. There was his date to think about. And what had Craig said? Andy was afraid of chasing the car down only to be told again to mind his own business. Maybe Craig had some sort of a business deal with the guy. Maybe he was an old friend.

Despite his doubts, Andy might still have decided to hop into his Volkswagen and chase the bigger car, except that fate intervened in the form of two fraternity brothers from Delta Sigma Chi. The three young men held a hurried conference in the parking lot, and they decided that Andy should not chase after Craig and Mary Beth.

They also agreed not to call the police.

"You just can't tell these days," one brother said to Andy. "We might just embarrass Craig if we call the cops. Maybe get him in trouble. Anything's possible, even with Craig."

If there was an All-American couple on campus, it was Craig Miller and Mary Beth Sowers. She was the girl who had everything — looks, a good figure, and talent. A business administration major, it appeared likely she would soon be promoted to a management position at the firm where she held a full-time job while carrying sixteen units at California

State University at Sacramento. She was also an athlete and an accomplished seamstress.

Craig was self-assured, personable, and gifted in his own right. He had already proposed to Mary Beth, and the couple was looking forward to a December wedding.

For all that, Andy Beal knew a person could never be sure about someone else. Even an All-American couple could step over onto the other side of the law now and then for an illicit snort of cocaine or joint of marijuana. Maybe that's what the ride in the Olds was all about.

Andy Beal and his girlfriend went to a pizza parlor, downed some beers, then adjourned to her apartment. He left about 1:30 a.m., still feeling uneasy. The picture of Craig's grim face in the back seat stayed with him. He returned to the parking lot and saw that Mary Beth's red Honda was still there. He got out and looked it over. Her coat was lying on the seat of the car. A white carnation from her corsage was on the floor near the clutch pedal.

Andy thought again about calling the police. Then, feeling foolish, he went home. He went to bed about three o'clock in the morning and awoke two hours later. The uneasiness was still with him, so he drove back to the parking lot.

This time when he found Mary Beth's car still in the lot, there was no doubt in his mind about what he should do. When a police car happened to cruise through the parking lot, Andy flagged it down.

\*　　\*　　\*

Charlene had driven Gerry to the dingy apartment building where he was currently living, and he'd taken Mary Beth inside at gunpoint. Charlene had followed them and stretched out on the couch in the living room as he took the girl to the bedroom.

For a while, she listened. Charlene had seen the fear in the girl's eyes when Gerry took her away. Lying on the couch, Charlene could hear the girl arguing and pleading. There was more arguing, then the sounds she expected to hear — the sounds made by a rutting male animal — the sounds of forced sex.

Charlene didn't hear all of it. She napped intermittently, awakened, realized Gerry and the girl were still in the bedroom, and dozed off again. During the time she was awake, she thought more about Gerry shooting the boy right in front of her. That was not part of the bargain. He had promised she would never, never, *never* see anyone murdered. And as long as she had not witnessed the actual killing a part of her could still feel detached from his actions. She felt betrayed.

Near dawn, Charlene awoke worried. Daylight was on the way and Gerry was still in the bedroom with the girl. Just as Charlene was wondering what she should do, Gerry emerged with a disheveled and dazed Mary Beth walking in front of him. He had a gun pointing at her back.

"It's almost light out," he said. "We have to get going."

Charlene could see the strain in the girl's face. Whatever terror she felt was overwhelmed by shock and utter exhaustion.

They went out to the car. Charlene sat in the driver's seat. Gerry, beside her, kept his eye on the girl in the back, his little gun ready for any trouble.

"Keep your head down," he barked to the girl.

Mary Beth obeyed, crying tearlessly.

Charlene drove through the back streets, protesting all the time that they had better be careful. She kept repeating to Gerry that the kid in the parking lot had seen their license plate.

Gerry wasn't listening. His eyes were bloodshot and he reeked with the stale, sour odor of a sidewalk drunk the morning after. Charlene found a freeway on ramp and turned east on Interstate 80.

"Where are we going?" Charlene asked.

"Just drive."

"It's getting daylight, Gerry," she protested, an edge in her voice.

The sky was turning from black to gray over the mountains. Soon, the sun would rise and they would be more vulnerable than ever.

Gerry watched the road until they reached open country. He then pointed to an off ramp, which Charlene took. They crossed a railroad track and drove into a residential court.

"Get back on the freeway." His voice was threatening.

Gerry saw another off ramp and ordered Charlene to take it. He then had her get right back on the highway going in the same direction, east.

Charlene could see the girl in the back. She was still sobbing softly.

Finally, Charlene took the car off the highway near Sierra College, a community college twenty miles east of Sacramento. She drove into another dead-end street. Gerry's voice was menacing when he told her to turn the car around.

She began to think again about Gerry killing her. By now, Gerry had killed a lot of girls. Why not her, too? He was through with the girl, maybe he was also finished with her. Maybe he was going to kill them both, dump their bodies, and drive back alone. Maybe he really was in love with Evelyn What's-Her-Name.

Charlene's only hope was that maybe he still needed her. There were many dark secrets between them they could not share with anyone else. In a twisted way this created a powerful bond. It also worked both ways. She must have needed Gerry, too. Otherwise, why had she agreed to see this sick man from whom she was now separated?

There were houses nearby, but only one was close, a large white residence which was off at an angle from the road. Gerry had Charlene drive a short distance further, then stop. He ordered Mary Beth out of the car and the two of them walked away, the girl in front, Gerry behind her with the gun pointed at her back.

A truck roared past on the highway and the wind rustled through the leaves of a nearby live oak. Charlene noticed that Mary Beth was stumbling a little as she walked over the rough ground.

Charlene saw lights shining from the windows of houses in the distance. People were rising early on the weekend, probably to go fishing or find enough snow in the high Sierra for a little early skiing. These were people who were alive and happy. Charlene thought about that. She also thought about wanting to get out of there. The big kid in the parking lot *had* seen their license plate. The police were probably searching for them now.

Gerry and the girl were more than a hundred feet away by then. Charlene saw them walk up a slight slope and disappear into some kind of gully. Then she heard it.

*Pop. Pop. Pop.* Three shots.

Charlene knew it was over.

Three shots in the early dawn as heavy trucks lumbered past, through the fading darkness toward the Sierra Nevada on Interstate 80, and Mary Beth Sowers was dead. Mary Beth, the girl who should have had everything, had lost it all in six ill-fated hours. A life was over so quickly, so permanently, so trivially.

In the car, Charlene waited, feeling both angry and frightened. The anger was directed toward Mary Beth as well as for Gerry. In a way she didn't understand, Charlene knew she had lost the competition with the girl in the silk dress. Even in death, the girl who was everything Charlene might have been had won some sort of moral victory.

Charlene was also angry and frightened because Gerry had been careless this time. He had been foolish and there would be a price to pay. The kid in the parking lot had seen the license plate, and he might have seen Gerry's gun. The police were probably looking for the Olds, and them, at that very moment. It would soon be over.

Her brooding was interrupted by the sight of Gerry returning through the brightening morning.

"We've got to get back to the apartment." Gerry climbed behind the wheel. "We've got things to do."

He drove the entire way. Once back at the apartment, Charlene automatically and efficiently started to change the bedding and to clean everything the girl had touched. Finally, exhausted, they both lay down on the same bed where hours earlier he had terrorized and violated one of Sacramento's loveliest and brightest young women. They fell asleep.

*       *       *

When Andy Beal finished his story in the parking lot, the patrol officer said, "Your friend is a big boy and his girlfriend is all grown up, too. People have to be gone for awhile before a missing person's report can be filed."

Andy asked exactly how long he had to wait. He was told the normal time is twenty-four hours. There were exceptions if the person did not show up at a place where he or she was expected, the officer said.

Back home, Andy called his fraternity brothers. He told them Mary Beth's car was still parked in the lot. They shared his concern.

Andy next called Mary Beth's apartment and one of her roommates reported she had not come home. He called Craig Miller's house and his mother said he'd not come home, either.

Andy waited until ten o'clock that morning to call Craig's employer. He was told that Craig was already an hour late for work and he'd not called in. Craig had never failed to call if he was going to be late, his boss added.

Andy returned to the Carousel parking lot with his fraternity brothers and one of Mary Beth's roommates. The young woman was the one who noticed the keys to the Honda lying under the chassis of the automobile, as if they'd been thrown there. That was enough for Andy. He went with the others to police headquarters and announced in no uncertain terms that he wanted to file two missing person's reports, *now*.

Detective Lee Taylor of the Sacramento Police Department's Missing Persons detail listened to Andy's account of the parking lot confrontation. The investigator was impressed with this over-sized, amiable kid's concern for his friends. The boy seemed to feel that he should have done something more when he saw his friends in the back of the Olds. The detective noted Andy's barrel chest and broad shoulders and wondered if the big kid would have been successful in stopping a kidnapping. But was it really a kidnapping that took place in the parking lot?

Detective Taylor decided there was real cause for concern. The case deserved more attention than an overworked missing persons squad could provide. The detective called Lieutenant Hal Taylor of the homicide-assault detail and went over Beal's story with him. In a few minutes, Andy and Detective Taylor were joined by Gene Burchett of homicide.

Burchett didn't look like a homicide detective to Andy. In fact, he didn't even look like a policeman. Young, fastidious, red-haired, blue-eyed, and wearing a vested gray suit, Burchett looked more like a stockbroker than a real-life Columbo.

Burchett sat down next to Andy and said, "Now, let's go over this one step at a time."

Daddy's little girl

Innocence

Charlene—twenty going on twelve

On the Oregon coast

The killer

The outlaw

Macho man

Between the Olds and the van

The wedding of Gerald
and Charlene as
Mr. and Mrs. Stephen Feil

The submissive Charlene

The van

Detail of painting on van

The macrame rope found in Gallego's Triumph

Charlene with Lt. Biondi, playing the role of investigator's assistant

Lt. Biondi with a possible murder weapon

The prisoner

The prisoner

Gallego lights up during his murder trial in Martinez

The father, Gerald Albert Gallego, condemned to death in Mississippi

# Fourteen

A solitary turkey buzzard rocked and tilted precariously on a warm updraft above the foothills still dyed golden brown by the long, dry summer which had given way to a damp November.

The vulture tilted a reptilian head and turned on wings six feet across, tightening its uncertain circle as it focused beady, telescopic eyes on dead flesh. The big bird dropped from current to current, descending down a vast, invisible staircase, drawing closer and closer to the motionless figure on the grassy shoulder of Bass Lake Road.

Up the hill and across the highway, the family in the farmhouse near the end of the road was awake. A man emerged from the house, took care of a few early-morning chores, then went into the kitchen for breakfast.

"Heard some shootin' last night," he told his wife. "Did you?"

His wife shook her head. She was a sound sleeper.

"Damned deer hunters don't care a hoot about the law," the farmer complained. "Can't wait until sunup to shoot. I'll be lucky if I don't find a dead steer out in one of the pastures. Saw some buzzards gathering above the road on the other side of the highway. Some people just don't have good sense."

His wife agreed as she dished up breakfast and joined him.

"Three shots," the farmer said. "Just three shots. Give a

fool a gun and he's liable to shoot anything. Thank the Lord it's the last day of the season."

Back on Bass Lake Road, a pickup truck carrying a pair of hunters, their guns racked in the back of the cab, rolled toward the refreshment stand at the lake. The men were looking for some coffee before starting their last hunt of the season. The road was bumpy and uneven. One of the hunters caught sight of a dark bundle at the side of the road as the pickup passed.

"Did you see something?"

"Nope."

"It could have been a bundle of clothes," the hunter said, rubbing still sleepy eyes. "Or maybe it was a body."

"Probably some bum sleeping off a bottle of Thunderbird," his companion said.

Hours passed.

A man and a boy walked along the road, idly enjoying the morning. As they approached the place in the road where Craig Miller had collapsed with a bullet in his brain, they noticed buzzards circling patiently overhead.

The boy spotted the body first.

The man trembled and drew the boy away. "We've got to get to a phone," he said, horrified at their discovery.

Overhead, the buzzards waited while an El Dorado County Sheriff's Department car rolled down the road. They circled and swooped, gliding comfortably on the updrafts, riding downward gracefully on an aerial escalator as another car and then another arrived. Not until Detective Sergeant Bill Wilson ordered the body moved to an ambulance did the airborne gallery break up.

Wilson reflected on what they'd found. The well-dressed young man had been shot three times in the back of the head. His wallet was missing. Robbery could have been the motive. The young man still had his wristwatch, however. Strangely, his shoes were missing. The crime scene, the sergeant noted, was not without strong physical evidence, as three shiny shell casings were on the ground waiting to be collected and analyzed.

It was a strange murder, the sergeant thought.

Almost an execution.

\*     \*     \*

Back in Sacramento, Andy Beal had told his entire story to Detective Gene Burchett. Before returning home, the conscientious eyewitness pulled a slip of paper from his pocket. "I wrote down the license plate number of the Olds," Andy explained matter-of-factly. Burchett ran a check on the license with the California Department of Motor Vehicles. The legal owner of the car, the report revealed, was a prosperous business executive. The registered owner was his daughter.

Since the missing college kids were last seen in the Olds, and a young woman was described as one of the accomplices, Burchett decided to pay a visit to the home of the businessman to talk with the registered owner, a Charlene Williams.

# The Father

*I made him drive off onto a side road and go a little ways before I made him turn the car around . . . I was going to have a good time killing this cop. Still he begged me not to kill him. He said he had a wife and children but I hardly even heard him for I had only one thought in mind, and I knew he had only a few seconds to live and that he would bother me no more . . . I made him start walking and he knew then I meant to kill him. He really started to beg for his life then, and then I fired the first shot, and walked over to him and put the barrel of the gun to his head and shot him again. He laid still after that, and I turned around and got into his car, lit a smoke and drove off.*

From the death row statement of Gerald Albert Gallego
Mississippi State Prison
Jackson, Mississippi, 1954

# Fifteen

One day!

Gerry had called and begged to see her for just one day, and against her better judgment, Charlene had agreed. And now, it had started all over again.

One day! Less than twenty-four hours with Gerry and now eight murders were ten.

By then, of course, Charlene was no stranger to kidnap, rape, and murder. If she were at all concerned with the immorality of the killing of Craig Miller and Mary Beth Sowers, this was by no means her biggest worry. Survival. Not getting caught. Continuing to live her life. Those were the prime issues on Charlene's mind. Eight people had been killed without the police ever getting close to them — except for Trujillo, that Yolo County detective — and she'd been able to handle him.

The last two murders were different, and Charlene knew it.

There had been that big guy in the parking lot. The one she'd slapped. The one she was sure had seen the license plate. Charlene was too bright not to know that if the police had the license number of the Olds, they'd put two and two together and come up with the right answer. The police would get on their trail and all the murders would be discovered. Charlene shuddered at the thought.

It was Gerry who had committed the crimes, she told herself. He was the rapist, the killer. She hadn't killed or hurt anyone. Not once. She didn't know, or wouldn't accept the fact that in the eyes of the law, she was as much a murderer as her husband. But one thing she did know about the law: A wife cannot be forced to testify against her husband. She found herself hoping that Gerry knew that, too. She wanted him to realize there was no reason to kill her in order to keep her quiet.

Neither Charlene nor Gerry had slept long. Gerry was very professional at times like these. He was proud of his knowledge of the police and what he thought they would be thinking and doing. He was always ready for them.

Charlene went back to cleaning every door, every piece of woodwork, every stick of furniture that the girl might have touched. They talked about the girl's purse. It was full of pencils and pens. Charlene couldn't understand why a girl going to a dance carried so many pencils and pens.

Gerry said they had to dispose of everything that could possibly connect them to the couple. Absolutely everything. Pens, pencils, purse, and the gun — most of all the gun, the little .25 caliber automatic.

This time, some of Gerry's arrogance, his indifference, was gone. She was reminded of those days when she first met him when he had been so polite and attentive. He was clinging to her even while he gave her orders. Not for a minute would he let her out of his sight. He kept close to her. Very close. Somehow that touched her.

Gerry decided they would take the gun and the things which belonged to Mary Beth and dispose of them in the Sacramento River. Ironically, he chose a spot called Miller Park.

As they drove to the park, he sat close. He wouldn't let her go. Even when they reached the park and were walking out to the little marina he wouldn't let her go. He held her hand and told her again and again how much he loved her and that he was never going to let anything happen to her. He was hanging on tight, as close as he could get.

The park was familiar to Charlene. She had gone sailing on a boat anchored there which belonged to one of her father's friends. Of course, that had been a lifetime ago.

They reached the marina and looked around for anyone who might be watching. There were some weekend sailors working on their boats. But they didn't pay any attention to Gerald and Charlene. When Gerry thought it was safe, they threw the things into the murky water. Then they drove back to his apartment.

Gerry left her in the car for a moment on the return trip. He stopped at the corner of Howe and El Camino near the Farmer's Market and went into a place that made doughnuts. He left her, but not really. He was watching her all the time through the glass door while he ordered some pastries. She knew that he was frightened, that he didn't dare let her go.

They took all the dirty laundry from the apartment and started to go to her mother's place to wash it. It was while putting the laundry in the trunk of the Olds that Charlene saw the shoes — the brown loafers Gerry had made the boy remove. They were protruding from a paper bag. On the way to her mother's, they stopped and Charlene threw them into a dumpster.

Gerry was angry because they had forgotten the shoes, but he didn't make much of a fuss. He just kept clinging to Charlene. When they eventually reached her parents' house, they drove into the driveway and parked. Charlene got out and began walking toward the back door.

"Hey, wait a minute," Gerry called after her. "We'll go together."

He just would not let go. Carrying the biggest laundry bag, Gerry followed her. A moment later, Charlene's mother was at the back door, her normally well-composed features strained and worried.

"The police are here," she said. Her voice was flat.

Charlene immediately thought about the warrant in Butte County. After all she'd been part of, her first thought was not about the ten murders she helped commit but about the sex charge against Gerry. Astonishingly, even her concern about the reckless murders in the past twenty-four hours did not make her think about any harm coming to her.

Gerry put the laundry bag down, turned to Charlene, and said, "Don't tell them anything. Just keep your mouth shut."

And he was gone.

Charlene had no time to pull herself together. She followed her mother inside. There was a red-haired man sitting in the living room, well-dressed with boyish good looks. Charlene thought he looked like someone who might have been a guest at the fraternity dance, the kind that the boy and the girl in the silk dress had gone to.

"This is Detective Burchett with the Sacramento Police Department," her mother said.

Charlene's father was sitting nearby.

As her eyes scanned the room she saw another man. He was introduced to her as Detective Lee Taylor.

Although Burchett was polite and soft-spoken, she thought he was antagonistic. Detective Taylor appeared to be kinder. She remembered how Gerry had warned her that if the cops ever questioned her, they would play a cat and mouse game. There would be a good guy and a bad guy.

"They'll try to trap you," he had warned. "One of them will be your friend and the other will be the bad guy. That way, they figure you might talk to the nice guy. Watch out for them."

She sat down and lied. She told the detectives she had been to a movie the evening Mary Beth Sowers and Craig Miller disappeared and after that had spent the night with her boyfriend in his apartment. She had not been driving the silver-blue Olds, had not been near it, she said. Instead, they had been riding in a red Triumph which belonged to her boyfriend.

The telephone in the kitchen rang and Charlene's mother went to answer it. Her mother called to Charlene that it was for her.

"Is it my grandmother?" Charlene asked, deliberately trying to sound innocent.

Her mother, standing in the kitchen where she'd taken the call, was hanging up the phone when Charlene came into the room. Gerry had been on the line, her mother whispered. She added that when she told him the police were still here, he said he'd call back later. Her mother kept her voice low so the detectives would not hear.

When the detectives finished their questions and left, Charlene's parents began asking their own questions. Her replies were angry and defensive. "I don't know what the fuck everybody is talking about," she said.

The bad language lit a fuse in her father. He delivered a short lecture about young ladies not using obscenities. Not realizing that murder was involved and certainly not suspecting that his precious daughter was involved in any crimes, Chuck Williams chose this time to remind her of the importance of proper language. The lecture ended when Gerry called.

With more humility than was normal for him, Gerry asked Charlene to meet him at an ice cream store not far away.

By the time she picked up Gerry, he was in a fit.

"We've got to go back up into the hills," he said. "We've got to move the guy so they don't find him."

*     *     *

*Lt. Biondi — Homicide*

In their opening phases, murder investigations are like a ritualistic tribal dance. Many people are involved; each knows when to come in and what to do. For example, before the body can be moved, searched, or examined and the cause of death determined, certain steps must be taken. The scene, like the one on Bass Lake Road where Craig Miller's body was found, must be "sealed," meaning that a restricted area is marked by a few stakes in the ground with rope and ribbon attached to them. Then the body must be photographed and the immediate area examined for physical evidence.

All of that was going on while Gene Burchett, unaware that one of his missing persons had been found, continued with his investigation. While talking to Charlene Williams, Burchett had made a few observations. She was blonde, attractive, short, and thin, just like the woman Andy Beal had described. After she'd told her story about going to the movies, the detective asked to see the Oldsmobile. She took him out to the car parked in the driveway. The first thing he noticed was that the car was virtually spotless inside and out. It was obvious someone had recently gone to great pains to spit-polish it. He looked at the license plate and saw that the number, 240 ROV, was the same as the one written down by Andy Beal. Even the blue velour seats matched the college kid's detailed description. Burchett knew there was something very wrong with Charlene's answers.

The red Triumph Charlene claimed to have been riding in the night before was parked in front of the Williams' house. Burchett wrote down the license number. It was then that Charlene told him she was getting an attack of morning sickness. She was, she confided, seven months pregnant by her boyfriend. That, coupled with a hangover, made further conversation impossible, she insisted.

Burchett terminated the interview after getting Charlene's promise that she would be available for further questioning.

Back at his office, Burchett ran the Triumph's license and came up with the name of its owner, a Stephen Feil, who gave the residence of Chuck and Mercedes Williams as his address. The detective procured a copy of Feil's driver's license photograph and stopped off at Andy Beal's place. Andy promptly identified Feil as the man he had seen in the passenger seat of the Olds.

Burchett called Chuck Williams and arranged for another visit. When he arrived at the Williams' house, the detective was greeted with a polite note on the door. They said they would be back in a half hour. He waited.

When Mr. and Mrs. Williams returned home, Burchett questioned them about Stephen Feil.

"Our daughter is married to him," Chuck Williams said.

"Really?" the detective said, wondering if Charlene had a boyfriend in addition to a husband. Why else would a woman lie about being pregnant by her boyfriend when she was really carrying her husband's child?

"We don't know much about him," Chuck Williams admitted. "He uses our home as a mailing address."

Burchett had left the Williams' phone number with the radio dispatcher at police headquarters in case someone needed to reach him. Midway through the interview, the phone rang. It was for him. He took the call in the kitchen.

Sergeant Bill Wilson was on the line. "Gene, I think we've got one of your missing persons up here off Bass Lake Road. A young man has been murdered," the sergeant continued. "His description fits Craig Miller's."

Somehow, Burchett wasn't surprised. After he hung up, Burchett went back into the living room.

"When do you expect to see your daughter and her husband again?" he asked.

"Tonight," Mercedes Williams answered. "They're coming over for dinner."

Burchett planned to interrupt the dinner and to pick up his prime murder suspects, Charlene and Stephen Feil.

*     *     *

Charlene and Gerry didn't make it to the Williams' home for dinner that night. They were busy trying to find Craig Miller's body.

They had driven across town to Highway 50 and back into the foothills where Charlene remembered the boy's body lying in the grass at the side of Bass Lake Road. But when they arrived at the spot, there was no one and nothing on the shoulder.

"Where is he?" Gerry demanded more urgently. "We must be at the wrong place."

139

Charlene looked at the roadside. It had been night when Gerry fired the three shots into the head of Craig Miller. Things looked different now. The countryside had opened up and she could see the brown hills with their undercoating of green and the farmhouse in the distance and traffic moving down the nearby highway.

Looking closely at the ground, she noticed that the grass had been trampled down. There were many tire tracks. Numerous cigarette butts and a couple of cigars had been extinguished on the pavement. The truth was beginning to dawn on her.

"Where is he?" Gerry asked again.

"This is the place," she said with finality.

*The body had been found!* The police knew the boy had been murdered.

Gerry insisted she must be wrong. "Take me to where he is," Gerry said, desperation rising in his voice. "This must be the wrong place. Take me to him so I can move him."

Charlene was irritated, but there was no convincing Gerry otherwise. So a macabre farce ensued with their driving to various locations in search of a body that wasn't to be found. Through the afternoon their desperate search for the missing body continued, with Gerry insisting that Charlene take him to the right place.

Finally, he changed plans. "We'll go back to the apartment and get out everything that might be suspicious," he said. "We'll get all the guns out, the boxes of bullets, everything."

Charlene drove back toward the apartment. From a block away, they could see the place was swarming with police. There was a police car in the parking lot of a nearby convenience market. Detective Burchett was sitting in an unmarked car near a gas station. Police were everywhere.

"Get out of here!" Gerry commanded. "Get the hell out of here!"

Charlene drove back to the mountains. Gerry had her stop at a shopping center. He entered the market and emerged a short time later carrying something in a large shopping bag.

When he returned to the car, he showed Charlene a light beige blanket. She asked him what he wanted with it.

"For the guy," he replied. "I want to wrap it around him when we find him."

They retraced their steps again, driving along Bass Lake Road, looking for the body that had long since been removed. Charlene still couldn't convince Gerry that it had been found. He continued to blame her for taking him to the wrong place.

Late in the evening, Charlene convinced Gerry that things had taken a bad turn. She reminded him that the cops were crawling all over their apartment. They were there, she explained, because they knew the boy was dead. They were there because they had the license number of the Olds, thanks to the big guy in the parking lot. It finally seemed to be getting through to Gerry.

They drove to a park in Sacramento. They stopped in the darkness under the trees and talked. They were there for only an hour, but it seemed like an eternity.

"What do you want to do?" Gerry asked. "I can go away for a while and then I'll come back and get you. Or do you want to go with me?"

Charlene was frightened. Deep inside, she knew it was over. All the kidnappings and rapes. All the killings. The kid in the parking lot took their license number and gave it to the police and now it was over. They would be arrested. What was next?

The gas chamber? She knew that was how California executed murderers. How did Nevada do it? By hanging? By firing squad? And what about Oregon?

Ten murders!

The teen-agers by Sloughhouse.

The kids at Sunrise Mall.

The girls in Nevada.

The little hippie in Oregon.

The lady bartender in Yolo County.

And these last two, the college kids. Yes, they would be the last.

Charlene turned to Gerry. "I'll go with you." What were her options? How could she go home? Where could she go except with Gerry? Maybe he'd still be able to take care of her — to protect her from people who would do her harm.

"I'm going to call Mom and Dad before I go," she said.

Gerry was the way he'd been earlier in the day — tender, affectionate, and clinging. He agreed they should talk to her parents.

They left the little park and drove to a bar in Fair Oaks, just east of Sacramento. From there she called her parents. It was about nine o'clock by then, and her parents, wondering about their missing dinner guests, were concerned. The Williamses promised to come right away. They asked her not to make any irrevocable decision until they talked.

When they arrived, her parents asked intelligent, soft-voiced questions in a dark booth in the back where no one could hear. Neither Gerry nor Charlene gave them satisfactory answers. They claimed not to know why the police had visited the Williams' house that day.

"The police are all mixed up," Gerry claimed.

"Whatever they're thinking, they're wrong," Charlene insisted.

The police search was bad, they went on to say, because of the Butte County warrant that was still hanging over Gerry's head. If it were not for the warrant, they would face the police and find out what all the ruckus was about. But the warrant made that impossible.

"The only thing we can do is go away for awhile," Charlene said. "The police will get the right people and this will all blow over."

Charlene's father was not sold. He said there was no need for Charlene to leave town, reminding them that there was no warrant out for her.

But she explained that Gerry was her husband and she had to help him and stand by him while he was in trouble.

Loyalty was important to the grocery store executive. He could understand and admire loyalty.

Eventually, the foursome came to an agreement. Charlene and Gerry would leave town for awhile. Mr. and Mrs. Williams had brought along some warm clothes for them — a ski parka for Charlene and a heavy jacket for Gerry.

They headed over the Sierra Nevada on Highway 50, past Lake Tahoe and over Spooner's Summit to Carson City and then up the Washoe Valley to Reno. They stopped in Reno and left the Olds in the parking lot of the Circus Circus casino.

"That's as far as we can go with it," Gerry told Charlene. He was all business again, but he was still clinging to her. "Call your folks and tell them to send some money. Have them send it to Salt Lake City."

By then, Charlene and Gerry had seen the newspapers and knew why they had not been able to find Craig Miller's body. The beige blanket would never be used.

Charlene was frightened by the amount of attention the press paid to the murder of the boy and the disappearance of his girlfriend. Craig and Mary Beth created page one banners. An outraged press printed every detail they had of the murder and kidnapping of the All-American college couple.

Charlene and Gerry went to the Greyhound bus depot and bought tickets to Salt Lake City. As the bus rolled through the night over Nevada's high desert, Charlene realized they had no plan. They were two frightened animals running in the darkness.

# The Father

*When I killed the cop, it made me feel real good inside. The sensation was something that made me feel elated to the point of happiness, for I achieved in putting to death one of my tormentors. After killing him, I wanted to kill some more. I needed money, so I drove the dead cop's police car into Mobile. I hid the car, and I waited in the Greyhound Depot until the banks opened. I got a cab and had him drive me to a bank and I instructed him to wait. The crowd wasn't too big, so I robbed the bank. After that, I had this cab drive me into New Orleans where I planned to take a plane to California to kill my older brother and also kill them cops that hurt me. But I was caught in Moss Point and while being guarded by two cops, I broke and ran, daring them to shoot me. They fired three shots at me but missed. I was caught a few minutes later and taken to jail, where I am now. For what I've done, I feel no regret or sorrow whatsoever, and if I die I'll know I was perfectly right in killing that cop. I honestly believe I've committed no wrong.*

From the death row statement of Gerald Albert Gallego
Mississippi State Prison
Jackson, Mississippi, 1954

# Sixteen

*Lt. Biondi — Homicide*

Though I didn't know it yet, Gerald Gallego was making mistakes. He was guilty of the kind of carelessness I'd seen in other habitual criminals. In Gallego, there was something more subtle at work, too. I believe that after his string of murders, he'd become so confident of his ability to avoid detection that he arrogantly began to taunt us with his game of rape and murder.

Yet, this does not fully explain his reckless kidnapping of Mary Beth Sowers and Craig Miller. I'm convinced that Gallego would not have attempted this had he not been drunk. Under most circumstances, even Gallego — egotistical, arrogant, and amoral as he was — would have realized the danger in nabbing two young people right in front of witnesses. Charlene realized the jeopardy in which he was putting them. But, as usual, she had been unable to change Gerry's mind.

In the previous murders, luck had been their ally. First and foremost, they escaped detection by the sheer irrationality of the murders. Nearly seventy percent of all murders in the United States are committed by a member of the victim's family, a friend, or an acquaintance. In each of these situations, there is a motive present. This is always the place where murder investigations begin. It is also the reason why serial murders, which are usually committed by strangers and without a rational motive, are so difficult to solve.

But Gerry and Charlene's luck went beyond the randomness of their crimes. It remained with them in the first eight murders. If the golden sunset had not distorted his perceptions, Brad Wood's description of the van that picked up Linda Aguilar — the opening scene of the drama in Oregon which ended with the pregnant woman's murder — could have been a vital clue. Also, like those of us in Sacramento still trying to untangle the disappearance and suspected murder of Kippi Vaught and Rhonda Scheffler, investigators in Oregon believed they had a prime suspect with a motive and opportunity. As a result, they were playing a waiting game, looking for the one clue, the single shred of evidence, the inevitable mistake, which would positively prove the young fisherman had murdered his pregnant lover.

Gallego made a mistake picking up Linda Aguilar in front of possible witnesses. But his luck still held.

Luck was even more brazenly on Gallego's side at the Sail Inn, where he carelessly nabbed Virginia Mochel in the parking lot. Only luck — good for the careless murderers and bad for Virginia — prevented Bill Cannon or one of the other regulars from checking up on the pretty bartender at closing time. For Virginia Mochel, a few moments one way or the other meant the difference between life and death.

In the Mochel murder, Gerald and Charlene were lucky in another way. The investigation of Virginia Mochel's murder was complicated by a large number of possible suspects. Investigators Dave Trujillo and Rick Mayoral could not overlook her former husband. And the froggers who visited the bar that evening were all a little worse for wear by the time they returned to show the bartender their catch. One of them had over-indulged to the point where he did not remember the last few hours of the evening or even how he got home. The off-duty fireman, called "raunchy and obscene" by one regular, had to be checked out, too. And in addition to the pool-shooting couple, there had been the sixty-five-year-old stranger, who by just being in the place that night and appreciating Virginia's looks found himself on the list of suspects.

Neither Trujillo nor Mayoral had been completely satisfied with their talks with Charlene, nor did they forget that
she and her husband, of all the people to visit the tavern the
night Virginia was murdered, had been fishing. The link, of
course, was that the pretty bartender had been found bound
with fishing line. That knowledge haunted Trujillo later, but
at the time, he didn't have anything concrete with which to
challenge Charlene's story. Nor did he have sufficient evidence
to convince a judge to sign a search warrant. After all, if every
person in the area who had been fishing the evening of
Virginia's murder was arrested, the jails of both Yolo and
Sacramento Counties would have been full.

With the Vaught-Scheffler murders, our case against the
young black counselor seemed convincing. He knew Kippi
from his job and he had been identified as the driver of the
maroon Firebird that Kippi and Rhonda were seen entering
on the afternoon they disappeared. Several people also
claimed to have seen the two young women riding with the
former counselor and a companion later that day. The suspect
did everything he could to point the finger of guilt at himself,
lying to us constantly about nearly everything. Though he
continually denied it, I found it almost impossible to believe
he was not with them at some point in the last hours of their
lives. I still believe that.

One of my top detectives, having reviewed the evidence
and having listened to the former counselor lie repeatedly,
wanted to arrest him and charge him with the murders of the
two young women. But I didn't feel we'd learned the truth
about the case. One reason was that there had been a small
detail in our investigation that disturbed me. Some credible
eyewitnesses claimed they might have seen Rhonda at one of
the stores at the mall *after* she was seen in the Firebird. If that
were true, our case against the driver of the maroon car and
his companion was indeed on shaky ground.

But finally, Gallego's luck was running out.

First, we had, as a result of our earliest investigations, some
solid physical evidence — evidence waiting for the right sus-

pect. The bullets removed from the bodies of Kippi and Rhonda had been fired through a gun barrel that had six lands and grooves and a left-hand twist. Lands, grooves, and twists in a barrel are scientific methods we have of identifying a gun. Each barrel is microscopically different, a counterpart to fingerprints in humans. No two people in the world have the same fingerprints, and no two barrels have the same microscopic imperfections. But frankly, the chance of finding the actual weapon which had fired the bullets that killed Kippi and Rhonda seemed remote, since most murderers get rid of such telltale evidence. Though I would not know it for some time, this evidence was to prove crucial later on in the case against Gerald Gallego.

Also, Gene Burchett's investigation of the couple in the Olds with whom Mary Beth Sowers and Craig Miller were last seen would not have been much stronger than ours against the youth counselor except for one important difference. Andy Beal had been alert enough to remember the license plate number. And, of course, unlike the black man in the maroon car, the man and woman in the Olds were the actual killers.

Given that one important lead, Burchett, a young but able homicide detective, would not be stopped. He did, though, have some help.

The night Craig Miller's body was found, news of the murder and the disappearance of Mary Beth Sowers was the top story in every branch of the Sacramento media. Miller, an outstanding student, was the son of a ranking executive of one of the nation's largest communications corporations. Mary Beth was the daughter of a nuclear physicist. A partnership in a Sacramento advertising agency was waiting for Miller if he wanted it when he graduated from college, and Mary Beth was already starting to enjoy executive status in a firm that originally hired her as part-time student help. Charlene had been right, these were special kids.

One of the more interested people watching the evening news was Chuck Williams. Even without thinking things over, he could accept the possibility that his son-in-law was a kidnapper and murderer. Not once did Williams consider that Charlene might be his accomplice. That hideous connection never even crossed his mind. Instead, he thought about the possibility of his little girl, his Charlene, being the next victim.

It was a worried Chuck Williams who called Gene Burchett and told him Stephen Feil's real name was Gerald Gallego. He explained that Gallego was using the alias because of a warrant for his arrest in Butte County as a result of a "family problem."

Burchett contacted Butte County law enforcement agencies immediately and learned about the incest and rape charges against Gallego. Checking further, Burchett traced Gallego's criminal record back to his sixth birthday. Included on the lengthy list of robberies, burglaries, and thefts were several allegations of assault, rape, and a variety of sex offenses. By the time Gallego met Charlene, he had been arrested twenty-three times and had served several years in state prison for a motel robbery.

There was no longer any doubt in Burchett's mind that he was on the track of the man who had killed Craig Miller and kidnapped Mary Beth Sowers. He was as convinced of that as he was that Mary Beth's fate was the same as that of her sweetheart's. Burchett was also positive that Charlene and Gerald Gallego were on the run. The investigator notified the FBI that Gallego, a fugitive wanted on a warrant from Butte County, had probably crossed state lines and was therefore fair game for their agents.

At last, the chase was on.

# Seventeen

In Reno, Gerry and Charlene were looking for what Gallego, still playing the role of the macho outlaw, called "the first stage out of Dodge." That ended up being a Greyhound bus headed for Salt Lake City. While en route to Utah, Charlene called her parents and asked for money. Her mother, knowing then that her daughter was suspected of murder and that she was traveling with a man who was in all probability a killer, asked Charlene what had happened.

"I just don't know, Mom," Charlene lied.

Told by her mother that she should give up and that an attorney would be hired to represent her, Charlene said she would soon do that. Meanwhile, she asked her mother to send money. Her mother agreed to do so if she would use the funds to come home.

Instead, after picking up the money at a Western Union office in Salt Lake, Charlene and Gerry continued their flight further east.

They went to Denver. The couple stopped off at a tavern for a drink, and during the interlude a woman's purse was snatched. Gerry, knowing they each needed a name change, had told Charlene to pick up the bag when the woman wasn't looking. As with almost everything she did, Charlene succeeded. But they barely escaped from the ensuing ruckus that developed when the woman noticed her purse was gone.

They stopped in Pueblo, Colorado, long enough to pick up new birth certificates. Pretending to be a pollster for the Republican Party, Charlene talked to enough people to find a man and woman with the proper ages. She and Gerry then went to the courthouse and purchased copies of the certificates.

Everything was going as well as possible, according to Gerry. He was sure that the Craig Miller and Mary Beth Sowers murders could never be pinned on them. "They haven't got anything solid," he assured Charlene.

Charlene wasn't so sure.

One thing did worry Gerry, though. A few months earlier, he had fired the same gun he'd used to kill the college sweethearts into the ceiling of the bar where he had been employed. The bullets were somewhere in the attic. He also knew he'd been seen firing the shots, and that spent bullets could finger him as surely as the gun, which he'd been careful to dispose of hours after the killings.

"I've got to get those bullets out of the ceiling," he told Charlene. "I may have to go back and burn the place down."

\*　　\*　　\*

## Lt. Biondi — Homicide

In Sacramento, Detective Gene Burchett was working tirelessly to bolster Andy Beal's testimony with physical evidence which would tie Charlene and Gerald Gallego to the murders.

Burchett's work was rewarded with a stroke of plain good luck. The thing Gallego feared most happened. A woman who had seen Gallego fire the shots into the ceiling of the North Sacramento tavern contacted the police. She was steered to Burchett, who listened to her story with a gleam of satisfaction in his eyes. She said the shooting had been part of a macho gesture typical of the savage little man. At closing time, with the bar practically empty, Gallego had fired several shots into the ceiling. His excuse was that he wanted to awaken a drunk who was sleeping at the end of the bar. What he really wanted to do, the woman said, was to impress her.

There were two such incidents, she told Burchett. On one occasion, Gallego fired a single shot. A second time he fired five shots. He had been worried after firing the five shots, afraid the marks in the ceiling might cost him his job. The woman had shown him how to repair the damage with a mixture of baking soda, soap, and cigarette ashes.

Burchett went to the tavern and the woman showed him where the shots had been fired. He then entered the crawl space between the roof and ceiling, located the holes, and, using a lead pencil extending from the holes as a direction finder, recovered five of the six bullets.

Burchett took the bullets to a criminalist with the California Department of Justice Crime Laboratory. After analyzing the markings made by the gun's barrel, the ballistics tests proved the bullets taken from the roof above the bar matched those which had killed Craig Miller.

*    *    *

When their funds were running out again, Charlene called her mother and asked for more money. Again, Mercedes Williams insisted that Charlene use it to return home and give herself up. Charlene agreed.

But this time, her parents took no chances. Still worried that their daughter might be Gerry's next victim, they contacted the FBI, which in turn notified Omaha, Nebraska authorities, where the parents were supposed to wire the funds.

On November 17, 1980, the day the money was due, FBI agents scattered themselves in the neighborhood of the telegraph office. The fugitive couple appeared at 11:20 a.m. As they approached the building, Gallego dropped back and Charlene entered the Western Union office alone.

Outside, agents quickly surrounded Gallego, and he was taken quietly into custody. At least one of his fantasies had been shattered. He had often told Charlene how his criminal career would end in a wild chase and shootout with police. Instead of going out in a blaze of glory, his reign of terror ended with a look of surprise and a whimper as the cuffs were placed on him.

When Charlene identified herself at the counter, two agents stationed in the office arrested her.

The couple waived extradition and, on the advice of an attorney retained by Chuck and Mercedes Williams, refused to talk to the police. A delegation of officers from two jurisdictions in California, including Bill Wilson of El Dorado County and Gene Burchett of Sacramento, traveled to Nebraska to escort the couple back to California.

\*       \*       \*

Four days later, two young men target shooting in a field near Sierra Community College in Placer County found Mary Beth Sowers lying in a shallow ditch. She was still wearing the blue silk evening gown she'd chosen for the Founder's Day Dance.

An autopsy revealed that she had been shot in the head three times, just like Craig Miller. Though the bullets which killed her were so badly deteriorated that a proper ballistics comparison with those taken from the tavern ceiling was impossible, an expert was able to match the ejection and firing pin marks on the three shell casings found near Mary Beth's body with those found beside Craig Miller.

The real police work on the macabre saga of Gerald and Charlene Gallego was just beginning.

# Eighteen

*Lt. Biondi — Homicide*

The arrest of Charlene and Gerald Gallego received my immediate attention. I was part of a growing crowd of law enforcement officials who had every reason to trace the couple's activities.

Dave Trujillo was more certain than some of us that the Gallegos had something to do with his case. Plagued by self-doubt, he kept remembering his two interviews with Charlene and wondered if there was any way he could have acted sooner. But there had been no probable cause, no reason why Mr. and Mrs. Stephen Feil should have stood out as suspects in the investigation of Virginia Mochel's murder. Certainly there were more likely suspects. Any single man in the tavern that night was a better target for investigation than the Feils. How many husbands and wives go around kidnapping, raping, and murdering attractive women bartenders? But Trujillo was now haunted by Charlene's parting remark when he had asked her how she was able to drive home while admittedly so intoxicated. "By the grace of God," she had said piously.

*By the grace of God.* They had kidnapped and murdered Virginia and slipped away undetected. And now, Trujillo was determined to build the best case he could. Recalling they had been driving a van when they visited the Sail Inn, Trujillo worked on locating it. Gallego and Charlene had sold it during their separation, but the investigator found the new owners. They showed him a bloody sheet and pillowcase they had found in the rear of the van. Trujillo also retrieved carpet samples from the van and sent them to the California Department of Justice Crime Laboratory for examination. Fibers from that carpet would later become vital in an investigation of another murder, although they were little help to Trujillo in his efforts to prove that Virginia Mochel had been another victim of Charlene and Gerald Gallego.

At the Sacramento Sheriff's Department, we were interested in the arrest of the couple because of the similarities between the Miller-Sowers murders and our own Vaught-Scheffler murders. But ballistics tests threw us off the track at first. Although all four of the Sacramento victims had been killed with .25 caliber bullets, the weapon which killed Craig Miller had a barrel with a right-hand twist, and the gun which killed Kippi Vaught and Rhonda Scheffler had a left-hand twist. Since the bullets did not match and we were still looking for black suspects, I initially doubted that the Gallegos were responsible for the killings of Kippi Vaught and Rhonda Scheffler.

Before the Gallegos were apprehended in Omaha, and even before Mary Beth Sowers' body was found, a meeting was called by the Sacramento Police Department, which included all jurisdictions involved in the Craig Miller murder, plus the Yolo County investigators and the Sacramento County Sheriff's Department. The group came together to settle jurisdictional problems which evolved when we discovered one evening's activities by the couple had resulted in a kidnapping in Sacramento and a murder in El Dorado County. We also wanted to discuss the multitude of leads concerning the Gallegos which were now pouring into the various law enforcement agencies. For example, there was circumstantial evidence, though not enough to go to court, that the Gallegos had murdered Virginia Mochel. Just how many kidnappings and murders were they responsible for?

Initially, District Attorney Ron Tepper of El Dorado County had filed a single charge against Charlene and Gerald Gallego for the murder of Craig Miller. Later, when Mary Beth Sowers' body was found in Placer County, a decision on jurisdiction became necessary. Sacramento became the logical place for the prosecution to proceed. Both El Dorado and Placer Counties could charge the Gallegos with a single count of murder, but in these jurisdictions there were no circumstances in the individual crimes which would justify either county asking for the death penalty. Proof that the murders were committed in conjunction with another crime, such as kidnapping or robbery, would be needed for such a verdict. We were not sure that proof was available. On the other hand, if Sacramento prosecuted, the accused couple could be charged with multiple murders and thus provide the special circumstances required for the death penalty to be imposed under California law.

All jurisdictions also agreed that Sacramento County, with a population of just under a million people and a proportionate tax base, could better afford the trial than its less populous neighbors. Facilities for preparing a case against the couple were also more readily available in the state capital. The Sacramento County Crime Laboratory would be available to the prosecution, as well as the resources of the California Department of Justice.

Throughout 1981, by employing a series of tricky legal maneuvers, Charlene and Gerald Gallego kept their mouths shut, at least as far as we were concerned. Charlene was represented by her family attorney, Gallego by the Sacramento County Public Defender's office.

Frank Dale of the Sacramento District Attorney's office launched an effort to build the case for trial. Dale, long and lean, an English import who became a citizen of the United States as a youth, became a key figure in the investigations which followed. He approaches the world with a wry, spontaneous sense of humor. But the keen intellect which provides him with an endless supply of sardonic, one-line quips also feeds a relentless desire for the truth and the logic which can find it.

Among those who looked at the arrest of the Gallegos with more than a passing interest were Richard Wagner, the District Attorney of Pershing County, Nevada, and Tom Moots and John Compston, who were alternately assigned to investigate the murders of Stacy Redican and Karen Twiggs in that state.

Almost two years would pass between the time when Charlene and Gerald Gallego were arrested and charged with the murders of Mary Beth Sowers and Craig Miller and the time they would finally face the court. And in the interim some strange and gruesome events were happening. On December 22, 1980, the bodies of Sabrina Gonsalves and John Riggins were found in Sacramento County. They were students at the University of California at Davis in Yolo County who were kidnapped near the campus and murdered after their abductor or abductors had crossed the county line. They had disappeared on December 20th under circumstances similar to the Miller-Sowers kidnappings. The double murder a month after the arrest of the Gallegos had a significance all its own.

In January of 1981, Deputy D.A. Jim Morris, who would prosecute the Miller-Sowers case for Sacramento County, called to tell me that the attorneys for Charlene and Gerald Gallego were calling for a discovery hearing involving the Gonsalves-Riggins deaths. Their claim was that since the modus operandi was remarkably similar to that of the Miller-Sowers murders, the same person or persons who had killed the two Davis students had probably killed Mary Beth Sowers and Craig Miller. Therefore, the Gallegos, who were in custody at the time of the UC Davis killings, could not be guilty of killing Craig Miller and Mary Beth Sowers.

Since that time, a theory has existed that I believe deserves consideration. Is it possible Gallego had underworld friends or a loyal relative commit the UC Davis murders, choosing the student victims indiscriminately, hoping to drag a red herring across his own trail? If that did happen and if that was his intention, it didn't work.

A three-week-long preliminary hearing was held in the court of Municipal Judge Edward Garcia. The purpose of the hearing was to decide whether or not there was sufficient evidence linking the Gallegos to the murders of Mary Beth Sowers and Craig Miller for a trial. At that time, Andy Beal's testimony was challenged by the defense on the grounds that he had been hypnotized by authorities during their investigation and was therefore not a reliable witness. Andy — big, intelligent, good-natured, and convincing — told the court he had thought the hypnosis "scene" was more or less a gag and that he was never really hypnotized.

When the hearing ended, Judge Garcia held the Gallegos to answer for the killings of both Craig and Mary Beth. The judge observed that he would have issued the holding order with or without Beal's testimony. To this, he added that he did not believe Andy had actually been hypnotized and therefore that his testimony should be considered valid.

Shortly after the preliminary hearing ended, Gerald Gallego, along with several other inmates, was involved in an escape plot. The plan was to go to the exercise area on the roof with the lone guard who normally took prisoners there, overpower him, and use sheets and mattress covers as a makeshift rope to descend several stories to the ground level in downtown Sacramento.

On the day of the planned escape, coincidence stepped in the way of the convicts. Several sheriff's deputies, rather than the customary one guard, accompanied the men to the roof. One guard would have been easy. But the prisoners didn't want to take on a group of them. Later, one of the prisoners involved in the plan turned informer and told about the plot. During a search which followed, strips of sheets and mattress covers were found along with a "shank," or prison-made knife, and a note regarding the escape. Frank Dale took the note to a handwriting expert employed by the Department of Justice, who compared the note with a handwritten motion Gerald had filed in court, complaining that he was being mistreated in jail. The expert said the handwriting on the escape note was indeed that of Gallego.

On July 27, 1981, Charlene, still represented by an attorney who was a friend of the family, contacted the district attorney's office and offered information, hoping to have bail set and her release from jail in exchange for cooperating.

According to her, she knew nothing about the murders. Gallego, she said, had left with Craig Miller and Mary Beth Sowers from his Bluebird Lane apartment and returned alone some time later. When he returned, she noticed blood on his jacket.

The story was rejected as false. Charlene, worried and confused, took stock of the situation. She had thought Gerry, like a true knight on a white charger, would take the blame for everything and clear her. When he didn't, she began having conversations with a lieutenant in charge of the women's section of the county jail. Charlene said she wanted to talk to Prosecutor Jim Morris. Of course, Morris couldn't talk to her without her attorney present. Charlene told the jail lieutenant that her attorney was part of the problem. She didn't believe him qualified to handle a criminal defense. Ultimately, Charlene contacted the superior court judge who was handling the pre-trial matters. As a result, Hamilton Hintz, Jr. and Fern Laethem were appointed in February, 1982, to defend Charlene against murder charges.

Bit by bit, the case for the prosecution was built. D.A. Investigator Frank Dale put together complete dossiers on the lives of the Gallegos. We learned that their individual journeys to depravity started from opposite ends.

Gerald Armand Gallego was born in Sacramento on July 17, 1946. By the time he was twelve years old, he had been arrested five times for burglary, twice for being a runaway, once for malicious acts, and once for vandalism. At twelve, he was arrested for committing lewd and lascivious acts with a six-year-old girl and sentenced to serve time in a California Youth Authority facility. He left the Fred C. Nelles School for Boys at Whittier in August of 1960. He was paroled from the CYA in 1961, arrested for armed robbery, and committed to the Preston School of Industry in Ione, California, on February 1, 1962. He escaped from the reform school the following month and turned himself in two days later. Paroled in Sacramento County, he was suspended from Sacramento High School in 1963 for "very poor grades" and equally poor behavior. It was about that time that he learned for the first time that his father, Gerald Albert Gallego, had been executed in Jackson, Mississippi, several years earlier for the murder of two men.

Later in 1963, Gerald married for the first time. His first child, a little girl, was born April 29, 1964. Eight months later, he beat his wife with a hammer. They were soon divorced. Three more marriages followed, all of them involving beatings. In one case, records show that he threatened one of his wives' family with death.

Gallego was suspected of a series of robberies in California. He was charged with armed robbery in Solano County, escaped from jail while awaiting trial there, and was promptly recaptured. Convicted of both the robbery and escape in 1969, he was sentenced to serve five years to life in state prison. He spent three years in prison, was released, and married in 1974 for a fifth time. By the time he met Charlene in 1977, he was separated from this wife.

An only child, Charlene was pampered by her doting parents and grandparents. She was an unusually bright little girl. Learning came easily to her and she participated in school activities and assumed responsibilities. But she was apparently attracted to a seedier world. Her grades began to slip in high school after she started experimenting with sex and drugs. She found it difficult to control her appetite for either. She was allowed to graduate only because she had the necessary credits. She attended junior college for a while but soon dropped out. Two marriages to weak men went awry. Her marriage to her second husband ended when she came home from work one evening and found him crouched in a closet, whimpering, obviously in the throes of withdrawal from heavy drugs.

Forever her father's little girl, Charlene moved into an apartment he helped her furnish and started dressing in new clothes purchased by him. He also bought her an Oldsmobile. It was about then that she allowed herself to be talked into a blind date with a man who worked in a card room. His name was Gerald Gallego.

Charlene stayed with Gerald despite his increasingly errant behavior. She became his servant, concubine, and finally, his Judas goat for a bloodthirsty murder spree which lasted more than two years. Obviously a poor judge of character, she had attached herself to a man who she considered to be strong, even though his courage never extended beyond the muzzle of his guns, the blade of his knives, or the extended arc of his clubs. He was violent only to women and brave with men only when he held a gun. He must have been afraid of Craig Miller to force him to take his shoes off and then shoot him in the back.

Throughout 1981, Frank Dale had been pulling together the last loose ends in order to give Jim Morris as solid a case as possible. With the bullets from the tavern to bolster the prosecution's theory, the case seemed very convincing. Dale and Morris both believed there was no defense against Andy Beal's testimony. And the damning bullets which had been fired into the ceiling of the tavern and their ballistic comparison with those which had killed Craig Miller really nailed the case shut. The prosecution was prepared to try the Gallegos for two murders. None of us realized the Pandora box of murders we were about to see opened.

Early in 1982, Charlene was assigned new defense attorneys. While interrogating her, they asked how she, who had never been arrested in her life prior to the Miller-Sowers kidnapping-murders, could be involved in as bizarre and violent an incident as this.

"That wasn't the first time," Charlene replied.

Slowly, she began to tell the story of the ten murders.

After listening to Charlene's story, her lawyers retained Cliffe Harriman, a retired federal agent who was operating as a private detective in Sacramento. His job was to verify Charlene's story. On March 2, 1982, Harriman contacted Captain

Richard Kelley, my commanding officer and an old friend of his. "I can't tell you much more than that ten murders may have been committed," the former FBI man said. "I've been hired to check the details and see if they really occurred."

Harriman then laid out the facts, though he declined to name the perpetrators. Captain Kelley promptly turned the information over to me.

Checking through the story, I learned that a crime spree started in 1978 with a double kidnapping at the Country Club Plaza. One of the girls' names was Karen. Karen? I wondered, or Kippi? As I poured through the details, I was soon convinced that Harriman was talking about our unsolved Vaught-Scheffler case. And I was sure we were talking about the Gallegos, who had already been arrested for the Miller-Sowers murders.

Lucky Burch, the detective in Reno, wasn't easy to convince. The story about the Judd-Colley kidnapping in Reno had been mixed up and confusing the way Charlene first told it to her attorneys. But the yarn had started at the Washoe County Fairgrounds.

"We had a couple of youngsters reported missing from there a couple of years ago," Burch admitted. "But we're pretty sure they're not dead." They still thought of them as runaways.

I noticed Harriman's still-unnamed informant had mentioned Gold Beach, Oregon, and I called there. After I talked to Verlin Denton of the Curry County Sheriff's Department, he accepted the new version of his murder case. What convinced him were the details Harriman had given about what Linda Aguilar had been wearing at the time of her kidnapping.

Dave Trujillo didn't need any convincing. He had been positive ever since their arrest that the Gallegos had killed Virginia Mochel. He also guessed immediately that the informant was Charlene.

The most dramatic of my phone calls was to Tom Moots and his partner, John Compston, the two agents of the Nevada Division of Investigation who had been investigating the murders of Stacy Redican and Karen Twiggs. (Originally it was only Moots who worked on the case. But soon after the investigation began, Compston became his partner.) For over two years they had tenaciously hung on to their investigation, traveling back and forth to Sacramento in the search for evidence. When the Gallegos were arrested for the Miller-Sowers murders, they were certainly alerted to the possible connection to their investigation. But without incriminating clues or, better, an eyewitness account, there was little chance they could prove anything. When I called to tell them their murder investigation might have an eyewitness, they howled from excitement. I suppose only a fellow law-enforcement officer can really understand the relief that comes when a two-year investigation nears resolution.

In Lovelock, Nevada, Richard Wagner, the District Attorney of Pershing County, and James "Kay" McIntosh, the sheriff, wanted the killers of Stacy Redican and Karen Twiggs brought to justice. The tiny city beside the Humboldt Sink has its roots embedded in the Church of Jesus Christ of Latter Day Saints. The predominantly Mormon community is deeply religious and law-abiding. An unsolved murder in Pershing County is unthinkable to everyone there, particularly the two men most responsible for law enforcement and prosecution. They had sought help from the Nevada Bureau of Investigation because it is impossible for a county with the geographic size of some states but with the population of a village to supply the manpower and money required for such a complicated project.

Compston and Moots found the two officials in Pershing County as different as night and day. Wagner, the D.A., dresses and acts like a Wall Street lawyer. The three-piece suits he wore to the little brick courthouse in Lovelock were pressed, fashionable, and immaculate. Of modest physical stature, the investigators found Wagner to be articulate, intelligent, and determined. They would soon find it was impossible to make an appointment with Wagner before 8:30 in the morning. Prior to that, Wagner, a devout Mormon and the father of seven children, would be busy for a half hour teaching a church school class. A conservative man who believes in the literalness of the Bible, Wagner needed no theologians to explain to him the meaning of "an eye for an eye."

Sheriff Kay McIntosh, as flamboyant as Wagner is straight-laced, wears western clothes and acts the part of a sagebrush-country lawman. He knows most of the people in the county on a first-name basis and even most of the strangers after they've been in town a couple of days. Six days a week, from Monday to Saturday, Sheriff McIntosh enforces the law in Pershing County with an iron will and an unyielding hand. On Sunday, he races stock cars.

Whatever their difference in lifestyles, the sheriff and district attorney had a powerful common bond. They both desperately wanted the murderers of Stacy Redican and Karen Twiggs — prosecuted, convicted, punished.

In Lovelock, Compston and Moots went over the details of the murders with Wagner and McIntosh. They visited the little grove where the bodies were found, looked at photographs taken, and carefully reviewed the evidence, paying particular attention to the cord used to bind the two girls. The binding was thick and heavy but different from anything with which they were familiar. With the information I supplied them, they began to trace Gallego's bloody trail through California, Oregon, and Nevada.

In California, the investigation was multi-pronged. From the time Harriman contacted Captain Kelley until early summer, Charlene's new lawyers, Ham Hintz and Fern Laethem, engaged in prolonged negotiations with Sacramento County Prosecutor Jim Morris. Her attorneys believed we needed her information on all the murders except Miller-Sowers in order to convict Gallego. Unfortunately, they were right.

The issue of hypnosis, which we thought had already been settled, came up again. Since the preliminary hearing in 1981 in Judge Garcia's court, the California Supreme Court had issued the Shirley Decision, which effectively barred hypnotic questioning as a law-enforcement tool in California. As a result, all of Andy Beal's testimony, including his writing down the license plate number, the slap in the face from Charlene, and the fact that he spotted Mary Beth and Craig sitting in the back seat of the Oldsmobile, was ruled inadmissible. Suddenly our case was weakened. Without Andy Beal's eyewitness testimony, the case against Charlene lost its crucial thrust. Now we had no choice but to make a deal with her.

The negotiations between Charlene's attorneys and the various prosecutors continued for some time. Eventually, and for some participants, grudgingly, a deal was worked out in which Charlene would be granted immunity from prosecution for most of the crimes. She would plead guilty to second-degree murder in the killings of Stacy Redican and Karen Twiggs in Pershing County, Nevada, and serve sixteen years and eight months in prison. The specific sentence was selected because it matched the time a California prisoner, sentenced to twenty-five years to life for first-degree murder, must serve before becoming eligible for parole. The agreement stated that Charlene must serve the entire sentence. There would be no parole, no time off for good behavior.

After the agreement was signed by all parties, Charlene began to talk to us. And talk she did! She traveled with us to each grave site, taking us unerringly to the places where Stacy Redican and Karen Twiggs, Rhonda Scheffler and Kippi Vaught, Craig Miller and Mary Beth Sowers, Virginia Mochel and Linda Aguilar had been murdered and their bodies left or, in some cases, buried. Her memory was amazingly accurate. Only in one case did she fail. She was never able to find for us the exact spot where the girls from the Washoe County Fair, Sandra Colley and Brenda Judd, were buried. And to this day, they've never been found.

There was a grim, almost ghostly air when we visited the crime scenes. Frank Dale from the Sacramento D.A.'s office, John Compston of the Nevada Division of Investigation, and I alternated as narrators and interviewers of Charlene.

We visited every crime site, from the steep shoulder of the frontage road beside Baxter, where Gallego had to lead his victims up an almost vertical bank before reaching a tiny clearing, to the grass-covered hills near Sierra College where Mary Beth Sowers was found.

Those sessions were all business, but Charlene's emotions varied. She would be on the verge of tears at one location and almost matter-of-fact at another. There was something eerie about the visits as the places came vividly and gruesomely to life during her amazingly detailed and accurate descriptions.

At Baxter, the site of their first crime, Charlene told us how she had waited near the general store for about ten minutes before signaling Gerald after the police car went away.

At Country Club Centre and Sunrise Mall, she was able to find almost the exact spots where the van had been parked while she visited the shopping centers in search of more victims.

We visited the summer-seared field near Sloughhouse where fence posts and power poles rose starkly from fields studded with tumbleweeds and dry, brown, wild barley.

Perhaps the grimmest of all our journeys was the trip northeast of Lovelock, where we sifted sand and shoveled the dark desert earth searching unsuccessfully for the bodies of Sandra Colley and Brenda Judd. There was an abandoned mine shaft near the place Charlene identified as the murder scene, and it, too, was searched after scaffolding had been constructed to protect us from its sagging walls.

Eventually, earth-moving equipment was called in — bulldozers and clamshells sifting the soil more gently than anyone would think possible. But we never found a sign of the two slain girls. There was, we realized, a good chance that hillside runoffs which turned to torrents during the exceptionally wet winters of 1981 and 1982 might have washed the remains of the two girls from their graves and scattered them across the valley north of Humboldt Sink.

The Oregon coast where the long, aging highway bridge crosses the Rogue River at its mouth between Gold Beach and Wedderburn rivaled the eerie atmosphere in Nevada. Stark, black rocks rose like mighty tombstones from the little bay where the stream meets the Pacific Ocean. We examined the crime scene under a thick cover of fog, moving from the road-side where Linda Aguilar accepted a ride to the rock-strewn sandy beach where she was buried alive. Traffic moved in a steady stream along the nearby highway, huge trucks groaning and grumbling, and it seemed impossible that Gallego could have committed murder unnoticed in open country so close to so much activity.

In West Sacramento, the attractive little sign at the Sail Inn caught our attention. Here we found a neat little bar and restaurant tucked away near the river, far from the busy motel row where most West Sacramento night life is centered. It was an unlikely spot for murder to be unleashed.

We visited them all and listened while Charlene made her statements, sometimes haltingly, at other times in crisp, businesslike sentences. I was struck at how eager she was to co-operate, to please us, to become part of our team. It was almost as if she had adopted us as her new masters.

Using Charlene's confession as a springboard, we were able to connect the Gallegos as closely to the Vaught-Scheffler murders as Gene Burchett had been able to tie them to Miller-Sowers. Remembering that some fibers had been taken from the bodies of the murdered young women, we asked for laboratory tests which would tell us if they matched those of the carpet taken earlier from Gallego's van. Charlene told us that Kippi Vaught and Rhonda Scheffler had been lying on red and black sleeping bags. Many such fibers had been taken from the bodies of the two young women. Fibers from the two sleeping bags and from the van's carpet were forwarded to a Sacramento County criminalist. The expert was able to match these with those taken from the bodies.

There was one compelling piece of evidence concerning the rapes of Kippi and Rhonda that Gallego could not escape. Years before the Gallegos were arrested, the chief criminalist for the Sacramento County Crime Laboratory had taken semen samples from the undergarments of Rhonda Scheffler. The samples had been frozen and kept in storage. Scientists had proven that semen and blood break down into the same components. Therefore, a sample of blood from a suspect could be matched with frozen semen. If there was no match, then the suspect was not guilty, period. But if there was a match, it would mathematically eliminate all those with different blood types.

I contacted the crime lab and asked that they conduct three tests. The first was a comparison with the blood type of Rhonda Scheffler's husband. It was negative. The second was with the driver of the maroon Firebird, who consented to the test when told it might clear him once and for all. Again, the test was negative. Finally, we tried a match with Gallego's blood, a sample of which we acquired through the power of a court order. This time the results were positive. Gallego was conclusively a member of the eighteen percent of the male population whose blood type matched the samples.

There was also the matter of the bracken fern. Both Rhonda and Kippi had vegetation in their shoes when their bodies were found. The vegetable matter, which included bracken fern, was all preserved and stored through the years. Before Gallego was tried and after hearing Charlene's story, we decided to check its validity as evidence.

Frank Dale contacted a plant taxonomist with the California Department of Agriculture and showed him the vegetation found in the girls' shoes. He verified the species of the fern and told me that it did not commonly grow in California below an elevation of three thousand feet.

Traveling to Baxter, we visited the area where Charlene said Gerald had raped the two young women and promptly found bracken fern. Then we returned to Sloughhouse, near sea level, where the bodies had been found. There was no bracken fern. Charlene's story of Rhonda and Kippi being taken to Baxter was corroborated by solid physical evidence that any defense attorney would have a difficult time trying to refute.

There was one more incriminating piece of evidence. Shortly after the Gallegos' arrest, gun registration records revealed that Charlene, using her maiden name, had purchased the Beretta that was used to kill Mary Beth Sowers and Craig Miller. We also learned that she had bought a .25 caliber automatic with the trade name F.I.E., which stood for Firearms Import-Export Company.

The F.I.E. weapon meant nothing to us at first. But then we realized, after Charlene's revelations in 1982, that it had probably been used in the Vaught-Scheffler murders. Frank Dale told me that Charlene had purchased the F.I.E. for Gerald in November, 1977, in a North Sacramento gun store.

I contacted a criminalist in the county crime lab and confirmed that the Vaught-Scheffler murders were committed with a weapon that had six lands and grooves and a left-hand twist. Next, I called the firearms enforcement officers for the Bureau of Alcohol, Tobacco, and Firearms in Washington D.C. He told me the F.I.E. had the same barrel characteristics: six lands and grooves and a left-hand twist. Finally, we had pinpointed the purchase of a gun which would connect Gallego to the Vaught-Scheffler killings. I was now confident we had a strong enough case against Gallego to convict him of killing Kippi and Rhonda.

Next, I procured a search warrant for the home of Charlene's parents and both her and Gallego's automobiles. A half dozen of us participated in the searches. The most significant item found was a ball of macrame twine found in Gerald's Triumph. It was a ball of twine which Charlene promptly identified as the yarn which was used to tie Stacy Redican and Karen Twiggs. Later, we traced the yarn to a shop in Sacramento. The investigators in Nevada took the yarn samples we'd sent them to a crime lab and had it compared with the twine used to bind Stacy and Karen. The microscopic and chemical match was perfect. Finally, the Nevada detectives had solid physical evidence to support Charlene's version of the Pershing County murders.

Preparation for the trial of Gallego for the murders of Mary Beth Sowers and Craig Miller was not completed until October of 1982. For me, those long months which extended over two years meant special duty escorting Charlene from one jurisdiction to another, from one crime scene to the next.

Again and again I was struck by Charlene's glee when her testimony was corroborated by facts.

We all agreed that the case of the State of California vs. Gallego, charging him with the murders of Mary Beth Sowers and Craig Miller, was the strongest. Therefore, it was chosen for the first test in court.

But just in case we would fail to convict him or see him get the death sentence in the more lenient state of California, we also knew that the evidence collected in Nevada was strong enough to convict him of the Redican-Twiggs murders.

For the sake of the victims' families, justice had to be served!

# Nineteen

In November, 1982, Gerald Gallego's trial for the murders of Mary Beth Sowers and Craig Miller began. For months, the Gallego story occupied front page position in the Sacramento media. And there is no question that the public was horrified and outraged. Therefore, to avoid any question of fairness, the trial was moved to Martinez, thirty miles northeast of San Francisco.

Like many trials these days, Gallego's dragged on and on. At times, the proceedings resembled a black comedy. Gallego, whose ego had distorted whatever shred of common sense he may have had, contributed heavily to the absurdity. He summarily fired the Sacramento County Public Defender who had been representing him and undertook to head his own defense. Now the attorney, Gallego loaded the jury with women. The egomaniac actually believed that his macho image would prove irresistible to women and would win him an acquittal. Prosecutor Jim Morris looked over the lopsided panel and used his peremptory challenges to seat five men so he could achieve some sort of balance. He knew that an all-women jury would give Gallego no chance whatsoever.

A last-ditch effort by Gerry to exclude Charlene's testimony on the grounds of marital privilege was futile. Frank Dale had long since found Gallego's second wife and had verified that her marriage to him was never legally terminated. As a result, none of the four marriages that followed was legal.

Therefore, the court ruled that Charlene Williams could testify against the man she once considered to be her husband.

As the prosecution's star witness, Charlene was under tremendous pressure to perform. To a large extent, her being perceived by the jury as truthful and not merely as a plea-bargaining opportunist singing for her life was critical to our case. But throughout the long ordeal in Martinez, she was a cool, devastating witness for the government. She was seldom shaken as she recalled, under the direct examination of Jim Morris, the gruesome details of each murder. Ironically, it would have been Morris who would have prosecuted her for the same crimes had her testimony not been needed to convict Gallego. Later, the jurors would say that, while they disliked her, they believed her.

Charlene's demeanor changed, however, when Gallego cross-examined her. As the following transcript from the trial shows, the two sounded like a couple in the midst of a domestic quarrel.

Gallego: Incidentally, when we were arrested, what were we doing?

Charlene: Picking up the money which my mother and father had sent.

Gallego: Before we were arrested, were you afraid of me?

Charlene: Yes, Gerry.

Gallego: And that was your . . . was that your motive for not calling the police?

Charlene: In part.

Gallego: After we were arrested, the physical fear was no longer a threat to you, isn't that correct?

Charlene: I guess.

Gallego: Don't you know? Were you in fear that I might physically harm you after we were arrested?

Charlene: I wondered about that, yes.

Gallego: (impatiently) *Mrs. Gallego*, are you ever going to give me a straight answer?

Eventually, Gallego succeeded in having Charlene admit that her feelings for him went beyond fear.

Gallego: Mrs. Gallego, you have indicated that other than this physical fear that you have another emotion, is that correct, that seems to be the restraining force, is that correct?

Charlene: Yes.

Gallego: Is this love?

Charlene: At one time.

Gallego: What time was this?

Charlene: It's been almost five years ago.

Gallego: So you haven't loved me since then, huh?

Charlene: Gerry, it was a love that turned into fear. Sometimes one outweighed the other.

Gallego: You have indicated to the District Attorney on direct examination that our relationship on Bluebird Lane was casual.

Charlene: By that point, yes, it was.

Gallego: Did you love me at the time of our arrest?

Charlene: No. It was more of a protection. You kept telling me over and over how much you loved me and how much you had . . . you would take care of me and never let anybody hurt me, which was just another lie.

It was Gallego's arrogance which sometimes added a comic touch to the trial. He strutted and posed before the jury like a cock surveying his hens. He was obviously enjoying the role of a trial lawyer handling a major case. Sometimes he was surprisingly effective, particularly with lay witnesses. But with the experts he would slip, damaging his cause badly. But no testimony could have been more devastating than the one he himself gave.

Putting himself on the stand, he claimed he had been drinking in a Sacramento tavern with Charlene on the night of the disappearance of Mary Beth Sowers and Craig Miller. While at the bar, he said he began playing pool with another customer.

"We were playing for shots in what they call a pony glass, which is an Old-Fashioned glass. It's three and a half ounces, which is a pretty good shot. The loser would buy two drinks, and if Charlene wanted one at that time she could have had one. But Charlene wasn't much of a drinker, you know."

Gallego testified he drank Charlene's share and eventually blacked out, according to his memory. Not until the next morning, he testified, did he remember anything.

At that point, Gallego could see that his testimony was impressing no one. Fortunately for him a recess was called. But after the recess he continued to hurt his cause as he continued to string his story together.

"All right. I woke up in the morning, Sunday, November 2nd, and uh, I was fully dressed with the exception of my shoes that Charlene had taken off. She had put a blanket over me. And um, she was — I had some cuts — I had a cut on my lip, on the bottom of my lip, and I had some bumps on my head and she was taking care of me. She told me what had happened the night before and um, she didn't tell me in detail, but she — gave me a pretty good idea.

"She stated that we had — that we had went out to commit a robbery and that somehow it turned into a kidnap, and um — she told me that we had — she went out — we had went out to get some money. That we — we were gonna take them out into the boondocks and drop them off, and that while we were out there we had proceeded outside the car. That I was armed with the F.I.E., and that she was armed with the .38. That um, we had — taken their shoes off to give them a long walk into town. And um, during that process, that uh, Craig Miller had attacked — had attacked me and tried to disarm me, knocked me down and that I had jumped up and shot him from behind. She — she told me that she had killed Mary Beth Sowers to cover the crime to protect me, us, and our future. Over a period of time, I had asked her extensively about this crime that we had done, mainly because I couldn't believe it and mainly because I just wanted to know what had happened."

Gallego claimed the murders had been committed with the F.I.E., the little Saturday night special Charlene had purchased for him late in 1977. But Charlene had told us about his throwing that gun into the Sacramento River after the Vaught-Scheffler murders in 1978, more than a year before the Miller-Sowers killings. Gallego's intent was obvious. He sought to discredit Charlene's claim that the Beretta had killed Craig Miller and Mary Beth Sowers, insisting the F.I.E. had been the murder weapon. And he wanted to distance himself from the real murder weapon, the gun which he had used to fire shots into the ceiling of the tavern where he worked, while at the same time admitting to the murder of Craig Miller during a robbery attempt. Legally, the circumstances leading to the murder of Craig Miller were irrelevant to his case. Either way it was first-degree murder. But somehow, in Gallego's twisted psyche, killing the young man during a robbery was more acceptable than during a kidnap-rape. Gallego also apparently believed that the claim of his being drunk would provide him with a diminished-mental-capacity defense.

But he didn't get away with any of it. We knew the gun which had killed Craig Miller had right-hand twist riflings. We could prove it was the same gun he had used to fire the bullets into the ceiling of the North Sacramento bar where Gene Burchett had recovered them. We also knew the weapon which killed Kippi Vaught and Rhonda Scheffler was equipped with a left-hand twist barrel. And we knew from the firing pin and ejection mechanism markings on the shell casings found near the bodies of Mary Beth Sowers and Craig Miller that both had been killed by the same gun.

Until Gallego testified, the prosecution had paid no attention to the F.I.E., which was irrelevant as far as the Miller-Sowers case was concerned. Frank Dale called the Bureau of Alcohol, Tobacco, and Firearms and was given the same basic information with which I had been provided. He was told an F.I.E. A-27, the same designation as the weapon Charlene had purchased in 1977, had left-hand twist riflings. Dale asked for the serial number of a test weapon which had been fired and was told it was forty-eight numbers below that of the weapon Charlene bought in 1977. Next, Frank discovered the same store that sold Charlene the F.I.E. had sold the weapon bearing the next highest number. He located the weapon in Walla Walla, Washington. Dale flew there, met with the owner, test-fired the weapon, and turned the bullets over to a ballistics expert. All three F.I.E. guns had left-hand twist barrels. Yet the students, Craig and Mary Beth, had been murdered with the right-hand twist Beretta belonging to Gerald Gallego.

Torrey Johnson was a key figure in the investigation. A criminalist with the California Department of Justice, Johnson spent countless hours making sure the shell casings found near the bodies of Mary Beth Sowers and Craig Miller matched. He even visited the plant which manufactured the ammunition used in the shootings. What he learned during these visits helped him explain the stamped defects on the shell casings which made them identifiable and proved they came from the same batch of ammunition. Furthermore, the defects were identical to those found in another batch of ammunition during a search of Gallego's apartment.

For what seemed like an eternity, the trial lasted from November, 1982 to May, 1983. Finally, the prosecution and defense rested their cases. Now it was up to the jury to deliberate.

After only three days of deliberations the jury found Gerald Armand Gallego guilty of the first-degree murders of Craig Miller and Mary Beth Sowers. The jury also found him guilty of kidnapping, a special circumstance which justified the death penalty.

When the same jury convened to hear the penalty phase, a separate procedure in California, Gallego had hired a court-appointed attorney, Richard Fathy, to assist him. Again Charlene took the stand and again she was cross-examined by the defense, this time by Fathy, who was going over the testimony of the Linda Aguilar murder.

Fathy: You got out of the van and handed him the weapon to kill her?

Charlene: Upon instructions, yes.

Fathy: I see. So you knew you were handing the man what he was going to use to kill Miss Aguilar?

Charlene: Yes.

Fathy: And you didn't suggest to him just tie her up and leave her there, did you?

Charlene: No. I do not tell the man what to do, Mr. Fathy.

Fathy: Mrs. Gallego, do you think that lady would have died on that beach if you hadn't been in the van?

Charlene: Yes.

Fathy: In other words, you think Gerald Gallego, doing what he did, could have been done alone.

Charlene: Yes.

Fathy: And you had no role to play that day?

Charlene: This is correct, Mr. Fathy.

A few seconds later, Fathy pressed his point.

Fathy: You don't think you are responsible in any little tiny part for Miss Aguilar's death, do you?

Charlene: Yes, I do.

Fathy: Tell us how you feel.

Charlene: That I didn't take a gun and shoot Gerry or something. What do you want me to do, Mr. Fathy, play God?

Fathy: Let me ask you a question about that, Mrs. Gallego. After June 1st or whenever this occurred, and between then and the day we started talking about Miss Mochel, did you ever call the police?

Charlene: No.

Fathy: Did you ever once take a thin dime and call a sheriff or policeman and say I witnessed a horrendous thing, a monster thing I cannot control?

At this point, Charlene seemed to lose her composure. Her eyes teared and she clutched the rail on the witness stand.

Fathy: Did you want to see Miss Aguilar killed, ma'am?

Charlene: No, I did not.

Fathy: Can you tell me one thing you did to help prevent her murder?

Charlene: (almost inaudibly) Not a damn thing.

On June 21, 1983, Gerald Gallego was sentenced to die in California's gas chamber at San Quentin Penitentiary.

Those who wanted to see justice done were *not* satisfied.

# Twenty

*Lt. Biondi — Homicide*

Almost no one believed the California State Supreme Court would allow Gerald Gallego to be executed. The record of then Chief Justice Rose Bird was inflexible. An opponent of the death penalty, she had found legal fault with every death sentence which had reached her court. There was no reason to believe Gallego would be the exception.

That consensus made Richard Wagner, District Attorney of Pershing County, Nevada, even more determined to try Gallego for the murders of Stacy Redican and Karen Twiggs. The State of Nevada, Wagner knew, was not inclined to coddle convicted murderers. They had just executed a convicted killer and there were thirty more murderers facing the same fate on Nevada's Death Row.

A governor's warrant was forwarded from Nevada to Governor George Deukmejian of California requesting extradition. Gallego's attorney challenged the warrant and his request for a writ of habeas corpus was forwarded to the superior court in Marin County, where San Quentin Prison, the famous penitentiary that hosted Gerald Gallego, was located.

On December 22, 1983, the Marin County Court denied the writ, making Gallego eligible for extradition. Richard Wagner and Kay McIntosh drove from Lovelock to San Quentin through a bad snowstorm in the Sierra Nevada. Even for

Sheriff McIntosh, a man with a heavy foot, the three-hundred-mile journey took seven and a half hours.

They arrived at San Quentin, hungry and exhausted, eager to gain custody of Gallego and head back home. But that was not to be. The officials at the prison denied them custody of Gallego. While they were fighting their way through the Sierra snows, the First District Court of Appeals in San Francisco had intervened and issued a stay of release.

On December 27, Sheriff McIntosh appointed me a deputy sheriff of Pershing County. I was provided with extradition papers and everything needed for the release of Gallego. It seemed that justice was boiling down to the ticking of a clock. And since Sacramento is less than a two-hour drive from San Quentin, I stood a better chance to race ahead of any further legal maneuvering designed to keep Gallego away from Nevada justice, if and when extradition was to be upheld.

On January 11, 1984, Prosecutor Jim Morris called to tell me that the appellate court had denied the stay of release, giving Nevada the right to extradite Gallego. Within minutes Frank Dale and I, along with Detective Stan Reed from my homicide squad, left for San Quentin.

When we arrived, the legal affairs officer of the prison was on the phone, already talking to a representative of the California Supreme Court.

Once again, they were trying to stop the extradition! The court's representative was asking San Quentin's legal affairs officer to stop us from taking Gallego across the state line. But the prison officer refused. He said he would honor any order issued by the State Supreme Court only if it were served in person by a representative of the court to a prison official. Until that happened — until the papers voiding the extradition were in the hands of the proper authorities at San Quentin — he would not stop us from processing Gerald Gallego out of prison. The California Supreme Court was located about one hour away from San Quentin Prison . . .

Now the race against time intensified. First, there were the forms — mountains of paperwork to fill out. It isn't a simple matter to gain custody of a convicted murderer. I looked at my watch as soon as our feverish writing was over. It had been two hours since we arrived at San Quentin.

Finally, the prisoner was handed to us.

Gallego and I sat in the back seat, bound together by mutual distrust. As is my habit, I was not carrying a gun. Gallego was silent.

We started driving toward the inner gates where we stopped for what we hoped would be a quick inspection. But that was not to be. An endless parade of little technicalities seemed to bog down our progress. Finally, we passed through the inner gates to the outer courtyard. Now, only one more inspection awaited us at the outer gates, and we'd be on our way. But once again, the slow, impervious round of bureaucratic formalities caused delays. I was drumming my fingers impatiently as Reed and Dale were signing more forms, this time to pick up their service revolvers. Any moment now I expected to see a vehicle of the Supreme Court climbing up the entry road.

But we were lucky. As soon as we cleared the gates, we wasted no time in hurrying toward Highway 80, the same Highway 80 that had been a silent accomplice to so many of Gallego's vile deeds.

Suddenly, Gallego spoke. "How are you going to like it being prosecuted for kidnapping?" he asked us.

"What?" I couldn't believe my ears.

But Stan Reed had clearly heard Gallego and he didn't care to hear more. He turned around and eyeballed the prisoner. "Shut the hell up," he commanded.

We had earlier anticipated that the Supreme Court would try to intercept us at Sacramento Airport with an order to stop. So we skipped the conventional passenger terminal and took Gallego directly from the parking lot to an awaiting chartered Cessna 310. We flew to Reno, where Richard Wagner and Sheriff McIntosh were waiting. They took Gallego to the men's room at the airport and removed his San Quentin chains. They replaced them with a set of hand and leg irons that belonged to Pershing County.

"There will be no funny business here," the sheriff warned gruffly. "You are now in the state of Nevada."

# Twenty-one

*Lt. Biondi — Homicide*

While Gallego was being tried in California, Wagner, Mc-Intosh, Tom Moots, and John Compston had worked long and hard preparing their Nevada case.

For District Attorney Wagner, the work involved was just beginning. A thorough prosecutor, Wagner was determined to get to know Charlene Williams inside out. Like a method actor studying a role, he felt that he had to understand the motives behind the behavior of his star witness. And like a Nuremberg Court judge, he needed to explain to himself how she could have taken part in all those hideous crimes.

Predictably, Wagner was taken aback when he first met Charlene. Prepared to see an incorrigible monster, he saw instead a tiny and timid young woman. On the surface, it seemed impossible to believe that she could have had any part in the brutal murders. Wagner soon learned that Charlene was as inscrutable and contradictory as any criminal he'd ever met.

He had to change his theories about Charlene several times. At first, he thought Charlene was a weak woman who had been pushed into the crimes by a dominant, demanding male. Later, he theorized that Charlene was a terrified woman who acted out of fear, convinced, as she must have been, that if she interfered with Gallego's obscene spree in any way, he would kill her, too.

Eventually, as Wagner began to understand Charlene's mind, he began to see how deceptive her demeanor was. Instead of weak and frightened, Charlene was strong and manipulative. She had only one goal: to become the leading woman of the strongest man around her. At home, she won the contest easily against her rival: her mother. Chuck Williams worshipped his only child, and she, loving the attention, catered to his needs and manipulated him to think of her as his leading lady. Although there was nothing sexually immoral about their relationship, Charlene became her father's surrogate wife. It was she who went on business trips with him. It was she who was proudly introduced on social occasions. It was she for whom Chuck would buy and do anything.

When she met Gerald Gallego, she saw him as another powerful man. On their initial outings, Gallego's manners were flawless. And later, when he started hurting her, Charlene accepted it. Charlene believed that her man, whoever he might be, should be the dominant figure in the relationship. Her style was to pull the strings subtly, behind the scenes. She would discover her man's weak points and use them to her advantage.

In the case of Gallego, she was by far his intellectual superior, and she knew it. She would enjoy the ease with which she could get good-paying jobs, while he would have a hard time holding down any job which required responsibility. A member of the country club set, she maneuvered easily in society, while he felt inferior to most people, especially men.

It's no wonder then that Gallego became impotent when he lost a job. And when that happened, his fragile self-image as a strutting, macho outlaw would shatter. That's when he would inevitably turn to his pedophilia, a sickness that is typical of weak men seeking power over the helpless. He would ask Charlene to wear pigtails and miniskirts and to lose weight until she looked like a twelve-year-old. Then he would demand that she arouse him sexually in any way, every way he could think of. But she would inevitably fail.

Gradually, Gallego's obsession with his impotence, his sense of social and intellectual inferiority to Charlene, and his chronic and criminal pedophilia created the underpinning for his murderous behavior. The short man who always posed for pictures, trying to appear taller, needed to feel like a big man, the type of man who can have any woman he wants at his command.

But for this he needed an accomplice. And he understood Charlene well enough to know exactly how to push the right buttons to make her obey him. Like a card shark stacking a deck, he set up a rating system and made sure that Charlene would never win the top spot, would never be "the girl with heart." No matter what she did, she *never* measured up. And Charlene desperately needed to win this competition with her invisible rival. She would do anything to be Gallego's leading lady. And she did.

That's how a ghoulish chemistry between Charlene and Gerald produced the ten murders which followed. Pushing each other's insecurity buttons, the lovers formed a diabolical combination.

Wagner knew that Gallego was perfectly capable of committing rape and robbery on his own. But murder is a giant step beyond any other transgression. It is the ultimate crime. That's why the more Wagner understood Charlene and her relationship to Gallego, the more convinced he became that neither Gallego nor Charlene would have committed murder had they not met and become involved with each other.

But there was more. Wagner also began to believe there was fulfillment of a sort for Charlene in these crimes. Involved in a "competition for love," she would fantasize that Gerald's sex slaves were part of the contest. Whenever they kidnapped two girls, Gallego would always choose a favorite. Inevitably, the one he did not favor — the one who didn't pose a threat to Charlene's position with Gerry — was the one who earned her sympathy.

As he moved through the scenario of each murder with his star witness, Wagner began to understand the gradual evolution of Gallego's deadly game. Initially, the sex offender would chronically complain that the girls Charlene found for him were "too old." However, this was not a factor in the later murders. Linda Aguilar, Virginia Mochel, even Mary Beth Sowers, were all fully grown women, not the children he had initially demanded. Wagner speculated that Gallego started selecting women closer to Charlene's age because he wanted to taunt her. Whatever truth might be in this, Wagner decided that the main reason for Gallego's changed behavior was more sinister. The age of his victims was no longer relevant. He had found the ultimate climax for his obscene fantasies of sexual power. Gallego's greatest high came from knowing that his victims would die by his hands.

Wagner also saw how Gallego's change in attitude toward his crimes made Charlene's position increasingly more precarious. Her role in the last four murders was reduced. The careful planning which had preceded the first six crimes was gone. Gallego began acting spontaneously, behaving recklessly. Charlene understood this all too well. Any moment he could turn on her. For her safety, she tried to be as useful to him as possible, always helping him clean away any incriminating evidence. For her safety, she also counted on their known intimacy. If Gerry had any rationality left, he had to know that too many people knew of their relationship. If she died or disappeared, he would have been the prime suspect.

Deep within, Charlene had to know that Gallego's reckless improvisation would ultimately ensure their getting caught. But in a childish and irrational way, she still believed that Gallego was powerful enough to protect her from harm.

True to his Mormon background, Wagner tried to salvage some part of Charlene's life. Thinking it was important that she keep her keen intellect active, he encouraged her to enroll in college correspondence courses. He was amazed at her curiosity and versatility. How many people, he wondered, would study and master the Icelandic language just for fun?

Her mental capacity notwithstanding, Wagner found an appalling flaw in Charlene's character. Both in Sacramento and in Nevada, Wagner had worked with the Miller-Sowers' prosecutor, Jim Morris, on the legal compromise that secured Charlene's testimony. Part of the agreement was that she plead guilty to second-degree murder in Nevada for which she would serve a sixteen-year and eight-month sentence. In return for her plea and testimony, no other jurisdiction would try her for first-degree murder, either as an accomplice or an actual killer.

But Charlene refused to accept her own guilt. Time after time, Wagner and others would go over the law with the young woman, explaining to her that since she and Gerald had planned the murders ahead of time, made preparations, and carried them out, she was, at the very least, guilty of being an accomplice. And each time, he would manage to elicit agreement from her. But within days, she'd end up right back where she started. "Why should I plead guilty to murder?" she'd ask once again, her eyes staring uncomprehendingly. "I didn't kill anybody." And they would have to start all over again. When confronted with issues of morality, Charlene would always escape to that same recess of her mind which enabled her to do nothing while ten murders were taking place.

Eventually, despite reservations, Charlene agreed to the second-degree murder plea. She had little choice.

\*     \*     \*

In May, 1984, Gerald Gallego's trial for the murders of Stacy Redican and Karen Twiggs began in Lovelock, Nevada.

Wagner's first obstacle turned out not to be legal but financial. Pershing County is huge but sparsely settled. The monetary drain of the trial on the county was heavy. Some community leaders even wondered publicly if it was fair to make the tiny population of this county bear the cost of trying an already convicted murderer.

But something unexpected happened. As a result of news stories describing the county's financial woes, contributions began to trickle in. First, they were mainly from Northern

California, where millions had been following the story for months. But as news of the contributions began to spread, in leading magazines and on network television, the trickle became a torrent of handwritten envelopes from every state of the union and, finally, even from abroad. Thousands of people, voicing the anger of millions of others over the lenient treatment killers were receiving, voted with their pocketbooks for the stern hand of Nevada justice. A total of $27,488, most of it coming in one- or two-dollar donations, was received by the Pershing County Clerk. These contributions paid for nearly half the costs.

The murder trial in Lovelock began. Fully prepared, Charlene did much to destroy Gallego's defense. Once again, the jury believed the petite blonde as she recalled the horrors in which she had participated. Following a six-week trial, the jury returned a guilty verdict.

Their deliberation lasted just one day.

On the morning of June 21, 1984, Frank Dale and I climbed into a county car in Sacramento and drove once again to Lovelock, this time for the last official time. We pulled into town under a cloudless sky a few moments after one o'clock in the afternoon, parked in a red zone in front of Pershing County's impressive little courthouse, and ran up the steep concrete steps and through the lobby into a crowded courtroom.

Gerald Gallego, his sport shirt open at the neck, was standing behind a small table on one side of the room. Richard Wagner, in his usual three-piece suit, faced him.

Gallego was speaking. There were no seats available in the hushed chamber.

"What you people done to me is wrong. You sentenced me to death with no damn evidence at all, nothing. That means that you've opened the door so anybody can be convicted and sentenced to death on the word of one person. That's exactly what you've done. You broke your own law."

A few moments later, Judge Llewellyn Young of Pershing County turned to the prosecution. "Anything the State would like to say?"

Wagner rose. "You bet, your honor."

After vigorously defending the legal system which tried Gallego, he said, "As a matter of public record, in this case in California, the defendant's father was brought up by the defense. He died for what he did, but at least he was man enough to stand up and admit it and recognize what he did. That hasn't occurred here.

"I guess the worst part of it all is to think that maybe there's a little bit of humanity, just a little bit worth saving. But it hasn't been shown, not even today. The great macho image hasn't even been enough to acknowledge it. There's nothing more to be said except to carry out the sentence."

A few moments later, Gerald Gallego was sentenced to die by lethal injection for the murders of Stacy Redican and Karen Twiggs.

It was over. Six years had passed since Rhonda Scheffler and Kippi Vaught were found by the farmhands near Sloughhouse. The longest six years of my life. Frank Dale and I walked out of the courtroom and into the little circular hallway which separated the main chamber from the offices which surround it.

The relatives of some of Gallego's victims were there, families and investigators mingling with each other, a little unsure of what to do next. Off to one side, Judge Young talked to a reporter quietly. It was a subdued scene. There was no joy, no jubilation, no boasting. Some family members appeared to be on the verge of tears. For almost everyone else — investigators, prosecutors, members of the various families — the feeling of the moment seemed to be one of some relief and much emptiness. Suddenly, it was all over. And in a real sense for the families, their constant involvement with their dead was also over. For even in the struggle for retribution there is some validation of the existence of the victims. Now it was over. All over. After half a dozen years it had finally ended.

I thought about those six years — the frustration, the feeling of futility right at the beginning when we thought we were so close to solving the murders of Kippi Vaught and Rhonda

Scheffler — only to be so far away. I thought about the feeling of relief, of an obligation fulfilled to the families, when Charlene finally cracked and provided us with the leads which would link all the murders.

There are still those who complain that we hammered out an unnecessary deal with Charlene. None of us wanted to give her an inch, not a single concession. But we needed to know the truth. We had a moral obligation to get the truth to the families of the victims. The loved ones of those poor teen-age girls in Nevada might still be searching for them, living on false hopes, if we had not unearthed the truth. So the deal was made and Gerald Gallego would die and Charlene Williams would live.

As for Gerald Gallego, some people, like Richard Wagner, think he might not have killed without Charlene as his lure. Personally, I think he was capable of doing everything that happened, with or without Charlene. He is a psychopathic personality with no regard for human life.

Together, they were effective. Terribly effective. And who knows? If Gallego had not been drunk and gambled on kidnapping Mary Beth Sowers and Craig Miller, they might still be murdering today.

The case of the People vs. Gerald Armand Gallego was finally closed. But I knew it would leave an ugly and permanent scar on us all.

# The Son

*I have the feeling that my father is inside of me.*

Gerald Armand Gallego,
to a court-appointed psychologist, 1983

# Epilogue

Gerald Gallego is awaiting execution in the Nevada State Penitentiary at Carson City, Nevada. He has nearly exhausted the appeals process, with only a final plea to the United States Supreme Court keeping him alive. Someday soon, he will be strapped to a prison gurney and injected with a massive dose of sodium thiopental that will cause his heart to stop beating. His death will not be easy. During similar executions it has taken ten minutes for the chemicals to take full effect. According to witnesses, the condemned are conscious until the final few seconds — and in pain.

Charlene Williams is incarcerated in the women's section of the same prison. She will be eligible for release August 17, 1997.

Their son, who is being raised in a good home and who was born after they were apprehended, seems well adjusted and happy. There are no indications that the boy has inherited all his father's sins.